Purchased with funds
given by

Florence Caplan

In Memory of

LEONARD H. CAPLAN

2014

Thank you for returning
your books on time.

Abington Free Library
1030 Old York Road
Abington, PA 19001

Bitten

UNIVERSITY PRESS OF FLORIDA

Florida A&M University, Tallahassee
Florida Atlantic University, Boca Raton
Florida Gulf Coast University, Ft. Myers
Florida International University, Miami
Florida State University, Tallahassee
New College of Florida, Sarasota
University of Central Florida, Orlando
University of Florida, Gainesville
University of North Florida, Jacksonville
University of South Florida, Tampa
University of West Florida, Pensacola

University Press of Florida

Gainesville/Tallahassee/Tampa/Boca Raton/Pensacola/Orlando/Miami

Jacksonville/Ft. Myers/Sarasota

Bitten

MY UNEXPECTED LOVE AFFAIR WITH FLORIDA

Andrew Furman

A Florida Quincentennial Book

Frontispiece: Port Canaveral Inlet. Photo by author.

COPYRIGHT 2014 BY ANDREW FURMAN
Printed in the United States of America on recycled, acid-free paper

This book may be available in an electronic edition.

19 18 17 16 15 14   6 5 4 3 2 1

LIBRARY OF CONGRESS CATALOGING-IN-PUBLICATION DATA
Furman, Andrew, 1968– author.
Bitten : my unexpected love affair with Florida / Andrew Furman.
pages cm
ISBN 978-0-8130-4975-5
1. Natural history—Florida. 2. Florida—Social life and customs.
3. Outdoor life—Florida. 4. Florida—History—Personal narratives.
5. Florida—Description and travel. I. Title.
QH105.F6F87 2014
508.759—DC23   2013038968

UNIVERSITY PRESS OF FLORIDA
15 Northwest 15th Street
Gainesville, FL 32611-2079
http://www.upf.com

For Rob Stone and Tim Lenz

Contents

Preface   ix

1. Introduction: The Field of the Microscope   1
2. Live Oak   9
3. Coontie   23
4. Fishing in the Dark   27
5. Accidentals Happen   33
6. Snooking   36
7. Neighboring Gardens   47
8. Burrowing Owls   60
9. Heat   65
10. Snail Kite   75
11. The Tale of a Cuban Immigrant   79
12. Geiger Tree   87
13. On Stealing Fruit   91
14. Spot-Breasted Oriole   101
15. A Trip to Venus   104
16. Painted Bunting   115
17. Squirrel Matters   119
18. Thoreau in Florida   129
19. Ivory-Billed Woodpecker   135

20. Bluefish   139

21. Our Suburban Screech Owls   150

　　Epilogue: An Evening Walk, December 16, 2012   164

　　Acknowledgments   169

　　Appendix. Florida Flora and Fauna: A Selected Checklist   171

　　Selected Further Reading   175

Preface

THIS BOOK TELLS A STORY about place. The place I call home. Florida. "The state with the prettiest name," as the poet Elizabeth Bishop wrote. More specifically, it's a story about my ongoing love affair with Florida. I write this book to honor the state's singular beauty, to express how crucially my contact with its land, and sea, and sky has informed and enriched the various dimensions of my still young(ish) life. I've lived here now for seventeen-plus years—longer than I've lived in any other place—yet I feel that I'm still in those early, passionate, and even sometimes silly throes of this love affair. As I'm not a Florida native, however, a certain defensiveness dogs me. Others, surely, hold a greater claim to speak for and about the various Florida phenomena that excite my imagination in the following pages. I beg these various others their indulgence as I forge ahead. Perhaps the meditations of this upstart Floridian might still be of use in their own way.

My wife and I relocated to Florida in the spring of 1996. I remember my astonishment at the ease and speed with which we traversed the states, from Pennsylvania on down, trying on various climates along the way as if they were clothes. Wendy and I have lived here ever since, and we have no intention of moving elsewhere, despite the lobbying efforts of some of our northeastern friends, who can't quite fathom our stick-to-it-ness. They've never expressed such sentiments outright, but I've inferred from the tone of some of our conversations (have I been too defensive?) that they just can't take Florida seriously. Our friends, I think—many of whom have relocated multiple times as adults—presume that inertia or sheer laziness must account for our longstanding tenure in the subtropics, that we're hardwired to hunker down. Or that maybe the heat has just gotten to us.

Such sour assumptions do not begin to explain our extended residency in this place. We have options. We'd pull up the stakes if we felt that we'd be happier somewhere else. But Florida, somewhat mysteriously, has exerted a fierce hold, stronger by the year. It may be that some people can identify the precise moment in their lives when they felt that they truly became Floridians—or Georgians, or Californians, or Alaskans, for that matter. I'd like to be able to make this claim, to describe the dramatic experience when I said to myself, Yes, this is where we will live. For me, however, I think it's closer to the truth that Florida has seeped into my bones, gradually.

It may be something of a cliché, this seeping-into-the-bones business. But I think it's as apt an image as any to describe the physical nature of my attachment to this place. That is, the moments when I feel most at home in Florida are those moments when I venture outside my home and office to make physical contact with the state's unique environment, whether an extended excursion with the family up north to see the biggest live oak tree in Florida (the sort of trip my kids have learned to expect in lieu of a Disney World vacation), a night of fishing one of the nearby reefs in the Atlantic, a quick jaunt to a local park or wildlife refuge to check out the birds, or simply those precious few morning minutes between breakfast and work when I tend to my garden of native plants and vegetables, which mostly involves the unglamorous, and endless (!), business of weeding. By this point, I have a fair amount of Florida dirt under my fingernails, salt-air in my lungs, visions of green stored away in my memory bank. This stuff accumulates.

Much of what drives our common culture today would diminish the centrality of homeplace in our daily lives. From the time we wake up, many of us are wired to the World Wide Web, often through more than one device, simultaneously. Through these smartphones, iPads, and computers, we access increasingly sophisticated and immediate information, and voices, and images, which go a long way toward dissolving geographic boundaries. I'm not immune to the various conveniences and charms of the Internet. Yet it's just as true that I've always found something thin and not-quite-right about much of what passes for contact, dialogue, "community," and experience, generally, on the web. My growing unease with the leveling force of the Internet partly accounts for the strong attachment I've forged with my actual, rather than virtual, place.

What this has meant, for me, is that in ways great and small I've tried to seek out and hold close an essential Florida to offer me ballast against the extraneous and dizzying confusions of Cyberia. Even the "Florida" that I encounter on the web and on the television is not the organic Florida that I seek out, daily. As I hope this book illustrates, foremost, there's something special about Florida's environment, a fierce beauty in its intemperate seasons and in the plant and animal creatures that accommodate themselves to the state's extreme moods: torrents of rain followed by months of stingy withholdings, tropical storms and hurricanes followed by months of placid calm, crushing heat followed by months of hypnotically pleasant warmth. I'd like to share what I've found with readers from all fifty states. My hope is that fellow Floridians might seek out natural Florida, too, and that those who reside elsewhere might also be inspired to carve out space in their harried lives to make their own local discoveries.

The Florida excursions that follow—some of them long trips and some of them short jaunts, physical and mental travel in varying degrees—represent an environmental memoir, of sorts, one tightly hinged to the social, cultural, and domestic implications of its environmental subjects. That is, my efforts to explore natural Florida represent less an escape from the social realm of my life than they do an essential outpost of my life as husband, father, neighbor, professor, colleague, and citizen. To put all this a bit more concretely, my foundering efforts to catch a Florida fish called snook put me in rich contact with fellow human and animal citizens I never would have known, otherwise, forcing me to confront race matters in America; starting up a modest vegetable garden with my son in our backyard taught us something we hadn't known about our Italian neighbors, and ourselves; the simple, yet indefatigable, efforts of least grebes and Cuban pewees to make a go of it in alien Florida cut through the noise of my harried life to reveal a more essential way of being in the world; exploring the long and complex cultural history of live oak trees in the United States, and in Florida, specifically, helped me learn my own place here; contemplating Florida's winter bluefish run offered curious comfort, and even instruction, as my wife and I coped with the unexpected high-risk pregnancy of our third child . . . and so on.

Here's one thing I've discovered that's worth passing along at the outset: it's not very hard to tap into natural Florida. There are small ways to do so every day, as many of us do. Camping at one of our state parks is great fun, but you might start simply by visiting your local park. If you're lucky enough to have a backyard, you can plant a small garden. Apartment dwellers might take advantage of the community gardens that exist in many Florida cities. During our cooler months, you might take lunch outside at the closest green space rather than in the hermetically sealed and over-air-conditioned indoors of restaurants, cafeterias, or, heaven forbid, your office or cubicle. Forgo the overpriced and over-air-conditioned fitness center and incorporate into your daily routine a morning or evening walk, run, or bicycle ride outdoors. You can simply step outside and look up! And listen! If you manage to evade the cacophony of our mechanized age (e.g., gas-powered lawn mowers, leaf blowers, edgers, hedge-trimmers, etc.), you might hear birdsong, the chatter of squirrels, the oak leaves whispering secrets. These are good sounds to hear. In his groundbreaking books *Last Child in the Woods* (2005) and *The Nature Principle* (2011), Richard Louv describes the concrete health benefits that accrue when we combat our "nature-deficit disorder" in ways great and small. If you're anything like me, and most humans, you might feel your blood pressure abate, your breathing slow, when you unplug for just an hour, say, and sit beneath a canopy of native Florida green.

These Florida years for me have been rich years in all the ways that matter. I doubt that the next seventeen years of my life will be more eventful, and neither would I want them to be. These touchstone events, mostly domestic, cannot be extricated from my simultaneous efforts over these past several years to know Florida, to touch its many sides. It's an endeavor that might occupy my attention for the rest of my days. It's a big state. There's still so much Florida that I haven't experienced. In a very real sense, then, the chapters that follow do make a case amid our increasingly impatient, itinerant age for unplugging for longer stretches of time, for monotasking rather than multitasking, and for settling down and staying put! The examined life, at least for me, has meant examining and knowing—or coming to know, anyway—my homeplace. The texture of my days would have been thinner, I believe, had I been compelled over these past several years to bounce around the continent like so many of my contemporaries, had I not been granted what I consider the great gift of time in this one special place, Florida.

I

Introduction

The Field of the Microscope

The question is not what you look at—but how you look & whether you see.

HENRY DAVID THOREAU, *JOURNAL*, AUGUST 5, 1851

WHEN MY SECOND CHILD WAS BORN, I lost my study. Not a bad trade, I re-alize, for my living, breathing daughter, Sophia. It's not a predicament I dared broach with my few, space-deprived Manhattanite friends. But it struck me hard at the time. Our mewling infant moved into the large room (which my wife insisted we paint pink, as if to add brass to the blow), and I was forced to make alternative arrangements. I moved my too-large writing desk just inches away from the too-large bed in our suddenly too-small master bedroom.

Whereas two broad windows graced the north and east walls of my former study, offering a vista I cherished toward my neighbor's sprawling live oaks, my desk suddenly sat before a narrow window, just two feet wide, which opened to a more shrunken scene, just ten scraggly feet or so before the wooden fence (rebuilt after Hurricanes Frances and Jeanne in 2004) marking the territory between my property and my neighbor's more manicured backyard. It's this change, this narrowing of my field of view for the hours a day I sit and try to write—but mostly gaze blankly out the window—that seems increasingly sig-nificant to me, emblematic of the life I have embraced in my postage stamp of Florida soil. Partly by accident, partly by choice, I have adopted a certain way of seeing down here in the subtropics.

The evolution of Henry David Thoreau's environmental vision offers an in-triguing model that's worth thinking about. In the years after leaving the relative seclusion of Walden Pond, Thoreau's field of view, ironically, narrowed even further. His now famous *Journal*, by the 1850s, begins to be taken up by increasingly close and direct observations of nature (e.g., tree rings, seed dispersion, squirrel shenanigans, anatomical descriptions of wildflowers and fungi). "I fear," he writes in his August 19, 1851, *Journal* entry,

> that the character of my knowledge is from year to year becoming more distinct & scientific—That in exchange for views as wide as heaven's cope I am being narrowed down to the field of the microscope—I see details not wholes nor the shadow of the whole. I count some parts & say "I know." The cricket's chirp now fills the air in dry fields near pine woods.

Heaven's cope. The field of the microscope. Thoreau had exchanged a view as wide as heaven for the circumscribed field of the microscope. He had substituted for the woolly whole intense knowledge of the details.

He had adopted a certain way of seeing in Concord, Massachusetts.

Captivated by this shift in Thoreau's focus, I concluded shortly after moving to Florida that I ought to look more closely at the place I called home and that I might begin with my immediate environs, an increasingly metropolitan swath between Fort Lauderdale and West Palm Beach. Neither quite urban nor suburban, but something hopelessly in between, it's a place scoffed at in equal measure by my friends living in the city and the country. Boca Raton strikes both cohorts as a shoddily constructed place. Hardly a place at all. Gertrude Stein's uncharitable appraisal of her hometown, Oakland, California—"There is no there there"—fairly encapsulates the prevailing view of most people in my sphere when it comes to my home of the past several years.

These people are wrong.

While human development (and overdevelopment) has left its indelible mark, an organic placeness remains here, and in so many other Florida locales. It only takes a bit of effort to see these places. In my town, it helps to live close to the coast, in what's now deemed "old" construction, rather than in one of the newer, homogenous, stuccoed neighborhoods out west. Here on the coastal ridge near the shore—rather than on the dredged, onetime Everglades to the west—developers didn't think to crowd out every existing sabal palm, live oak, slash pine, and palmetto frond to maximize every square foot "under air," in real-estate parlance. Just enough scrubby land and waterway remain for gopher tortoises, raccoons, opossums, skunks, squirrels, armadillos, lizards, and ospreys, and numerous other birds, to make a go of it in the eastern stretches of my town. One virtue of the human cohort here is that we tend to go to bed early, relinquishing the terrain to these and plenty of other animal residents. Screech owls make occasional nighttime appearances on my mailbox and on the jutting hurricane shutter frame on my neighbor's second-floor window; burrowing owls hunt around their nests on the undeveloped parcels of the college campus at which I work; I've been startled on more than one occasion by the sight of a dusty fox darting across my headlights in the middle of what we call "downtown."

Most significantly to me (a bird-watcher), my home stands on what must be a primordial coastal migratory route for countless songbird species that split their time between the tropics of Central and South America and the wooded northeast of the United States and Canada's boreal forest. Dry-season avian residents stay longer, while a precious handful of year-round resident birds (cardinals, red-bellied woodpeckers, spot-breasted orioles, mourning doves, etc.) thankfully remain to keep us company during the wet season. These are our only south Florida seasons—wet and dry—as Marjory Stoneman Douglas observes in her classic, *The Everglades: River of Grass* (1947).

Short of ceding my small property to my feathered neighbors, I've tried to accommodate their preferences. After taking up residence, I installed a water dripper and a small wading pond in the backyard, harnessing every ounce of my impoverished engineering skills. A bird feeder was easier to install and goes a long way each dry season toward meeting the caloric requirements of our painted bunting flock (plus nearly every squirrel in our neighborhood). Roger Tory Peterson dubbed the painted bunting "the most gaudily colored North American songbird," and the males do appear dipped in gaudy hues of blue, green, and red. The buntings flit off in April or May to their more northerly breeding sites without so much as a seeyalater, but the cardinals feast year-round on the seeds, as do the red-bellied woodpeckers, which don't quite fit inside the "squirrel-proof" caging. They dangle precariously from the feeder, poking their scarlet-dabbed heads inside for bits of fruit and nuts.

Over the years, Wendy and I have planted numerous native plants and trees, most productively a grove of firebush, which boasts meaty berries and fist-fuls of slender, orange flower cones. Ruby-throated hummingbirds and spot-breasted orioles savor the nectar, as do the butterflies monarch, giant swallow-tail, gold-rimmed swallowtail, zebra longwing (Florida's state butterfly), gulf fritillary, julia, cloudless sulphur, ruddy daggerwing, atala, and various others I haven't yet identified. Smaller airborne insects and crawling bugs must also appreciate the flowers, judging from the menagerie of tiny warblers that flit about the branches in pursuit of them during the dry season and from the full-time resident cardinals that more deliberately hop from perch to perch stalking their quarry. These seed-eaters apparently eat more insects than most people realize. Bees, too, dance whirligig in abundance about the firebush, which especially cheers me given reports of their rapid demise. The ubiquitous mockingbirds (Florida's state bird) relish the firebush berries, and volunteer firebush sprigs all about the backyard betray their haphazard droppings.

I can't claim to see much of my yard's flora and fauna from the narrow vantage point behind my computer monitor. For one thing, the bird feeder and dripper in the backyard lay well beyond my field of view. Same goes for the necklace pod and plumbago shrubs out front, the twin sabal palms and live oaks, and the generous orange blossoms and broad leaves of my geiger tree, the tree which served John James Audubon well as the backdrop for his canoodling white-crowned pigeons of the Keys. Instead, what lies immediately outside my study window before the wooden fence is the outside edge of my lime tree and one of my firebush shrubs, a flat ground of sandy dirt and low-lying weeds between the plantings. And so I don't see most of the daytime activity buzzing about the property. But it's fairly amazing how much I *do* manage to see from this narrow, even magnified, vista. To enhance the view, I've removed the window's dusty screen, which contributed an unacceptable haze. I've logged a good number of hours gazing out this narrow window when I properly should be writing (or at least doing the laundry), so much time that Sophia, no longer that mewling infant, recently offered me her own version of an Audubon painting: two birds on a branch of our lime tree, a cardinal and another impressively rendered but indeterminate species. The cardinal looks toward the mystery bird, but the mystery bird looks straight toward the viewer, me. A thought-bubble above the bird challenges me with the query, "WHAT ARE YOU LOOKIN' AT?" It may be that my daughter has grown impatient with her hopelessly dazed and distracted father.

My favorite time to look outside my narrow window is right around the federal tax deadline in April. It's a bittersweet time each year as the yard suddenly pulses with life—migration in full swing—but will just as suddenly grow pretty quiet for the long wet season. The painted buntings, if they're still around by tax day, will soon be leaving for six months or so. It's June now as I write these lines. The last bunting, a pale green female, vanished weeks ago. "It's sad here without them," my wife declared the other day from our kitchen, gazing out our sliding glass door toward the abandoned feeder. I wanted to tell her to take heart, that the buntings would be back soon enough, but these are August and September sentiments. It's only June. "Yes," I confessed. "It's a little sad."

For a while now, I've kept tattered migration notes, marking the avian comings and goings outside. Little more than a list, really. Here's what I saw from my window the morning of one recent tax day:

> pair of black-throated blues
> lots of redstarts
> cardinals
> JAGs
> common yellowthroat
> buntings all over the place
> palms, bunch
> ovenbird!
> blue jays
> doves, Eurasian, white-winged, mourning
> northern parula??

That's what I'm lookin' at! to answer the question posed by Sophia's saucy mystery bird. The warblers outside my study window routinely flutter within the lime tree and firebush branches hunting airborne insects. Redstarts, the males dappled in fire-orange and black paint, each year come early and stay late during spring migration, so it's no surprise that I saw "lots" on April 15. They have a distinct way of fanning their tails, swishing them back and forth as they scoot from branch to branch, making even the gray females easy to identify. (It's impolitic to say, I realize, but most female birds truly are duller in appearance.) Even more prevalent than the redstarts are the palm warblers, who hang around all season in their dusty, dry-season clothes, bobbing their tails. More scarce are the compact and chunky black-throated blues. The male boasts a midnight-blue cap and back, which contrast starkly with the black throat and sides that, in turn, give way sharply to a white belly. Finally, the ovenbird, as my exclamation point above probably suggests, is a bird whose presence I particularly savor. It's one of the few "shout" birds in my home—worth a shout, that is, to whomever else happens to be around at the time so that they might hurry over and see it through the window, too. (JAG, by contrast, is my shorthand for "just a grackle.")

It's not a particularly rare bird, the ovenbird. It's a singer "everyone has heard," Robert Frost claims in his 1916 poem devoted to the creature, maybe overstating the case. Still, the persistent, midsummer song of the ovenbird provokes wistfulness in Frost. "The question that he frames in all but words/," the poet concludes, "Is what to make of a diminished thing." Even though I keep my window open, I haven't heard the ovenbird's purportedly emphatic song (*TEACHER-TEACHER-TEACHER!*) and rarely do I hear other warbler songs, mostly because they don't start singing in earnest until they reach their breeding grounds in Frost's New England, and elsewhere. But the ovenbird invariably puts me in a wistful mood, too. I think I've figured out why; for while I typically spot other migrants in pairs or even groups, I've only ever spotted single ovenbirds and tend even to think about them in the singular. It walks gingerly on the ground outside my window, turning over leaves and sticks in search of food, bobbing its brick-red, mohawk-striped head. Rarely have I seen it fly. One would think that the ovenbird walks all the way to and from South America and New Hampshire each year. There's something about spotting this solitary bird. No matter how many times I see that telltale mohawk, no matter how many ovenbirds I must be seeing each season, it always *seems* like I'm seeing the same one, the last one. Frost was right. The ovenbird does encourage one to contemplate diminished things.

I've come to think of the narrow view from my study window as my own makeshift version of an ornithologist's moon, which they train their spotting scopes upon at night to track the nocturnal migration of birds. Recording the number and even the size and trajectory of the bird silhouettes that flit across the moon's bright field gives ornithologists a pretty good sense of the goings on. Looking outside my window, I don't see as much as I do when I head outside, but I think that I, too, glean a pretty fair sense of what's out there. And I don't spook anything from behind my window. On this particular morning in June, I haven't seen a whole heck of a lot, to be perfectly honest. A Eurasian collared dove trekked lazily on the ground, left to right across my field of view, bobbing its head. A small lizard performed an impressive set of pushups on the skeletal firebush branches, which I've recently pruned. A blue jay (I think) flitted across my field of view.

It's a little sad now.

All the same, paying close attention out my window during the seasons, wet and dry, is one of the ways that I'm finally beginning to know this place after all these years. Its rhythms. To know a place, to know it deeply, is to notice the small changes. And so I've taken notice that large curly-tailed lizards seem to be taking over my neighborhood; that brown thrashers continue to make their itinerant appearances at roughly the same rate; that I rarely see the chestnut cheeks anymore of Cape May warblers coming through during migration; that the burly, invasive marine toads have nearly displaced the more tender skin-and-bone frogs, which still chirp during occasional magical nights. Most disconcertingly, given my avian sympathies, I used to see whole flocks of small common ground doves out my study window but don't anymore. They'd take to the air in a great flurry, bleating volubly, their wings flashing rust. The wing-beats, I've learned, actually produce the bleating sound. Now, as if standing in for these tiny doves, larger white-winged doves have emerged and seem to be thriving.

How am I supposed to feel about the few, and fewer, and finally disappearing common ground doves and about these emergent white-winged doves? It's tough to see the avian ledger as balanced. The native common ground doves, while still fairly abundant statewide, appear to be in decline, by most reports, on account of urbanization and habitat destruction. The thriving white-winged doves aren't native to the area but were introduced from the western states in the 1970s when a local aviary released a large flock. The increasingly constructed Florida landscape apparently agrees with them. As much as I appreciate the flash of white as these new doves flit off outside my window, I find myself missing in far greater measure the flash of rust from the common ground doves, their fevered bleatings. I pine for these vanished birds.

It's a little sad.

Thoreau's way of being and seeing in the world, his up-close efforts to know his place, makes more and more sense to me the longer I hunker down in my adopted home state of Florida. The competing influence of e-mail and the Internet—the World Wide Web—only intensifies my resolve to train my eyes upon the actual, local realm. Why banish ourselves to Cyberia?

I don't mean to overstate the case. I use and appreciate the Internet, as I've stated earlier. I'm old enough to remember what it was like to conduct research and send letters the old-fashioned way. It's great, thrilling even, to have so much information accessible at my fingertips, to communicate online instantaneously with colleagues and friends across the globe (barring technical difficulty). All the same, there's an unfortunate corollary to being anywhere at any time. To be anywhere, in a certain way, is also—in a way just as real—to be nowhere. I'm not sure how many others feel this way, or feel that it's a problem. Here I risk striking a preachy, maybe even condescending, chord, but I worry that place matters less and less to more and more people, largely on account of the Internet. I worry that some of the technologies that offer access to an increasingly dazzling virtual environment threaten to preclude our immersion, and emotional investment, in the actual environment. I worry that all manner of wondrous plants and animals disappear these days without anyone really noticing or thinking it's a little sad. And despite all my bluster, I worry that I've given over too many of my own minutes and hours to the web. In short, I worry that I'm part of the problem.

Something tells me that I ought to resist the enticements of the web more concertedly. The hazy breadth and dizzying speed of my daily transactions online only intensify my visceral need to make physical contact with the actual world outside my window, beyond the small, square border of my computer screen. There's so much I haven't seen so near at hand in this place called Florida, things not only terrestrial but also aquatic. Like this local fish I've only just heard about. Snook. The name sounds almost apocryphal, but the species exists! It's an inshore fish that has inhabited our inlets and estuaries, our inshore creeks and canals, since Florida's primordial days. Have you seen one? I haven't. I want to know snook. I want to see one. Up-close. And I will.

One can glimpse the heavens, perhaps, through the field of a microscope.

2

Live Oak

I STUMBLED ACROSS A NEW LIVE OAK the other day on my college campus, which caught me by surprise and started me thinking in earnest about these once-prolific Florida trees. I was minding my own business, walking back to my office along my usual route after administering my last final exam of the semester. I walk fast, and so the rubber soles of my shoes actually skidded on the cement sidewalk on the quad as I halted alongside this arboreal surprise. There we stood, shoulder to shoulder. I was so stunned by the sudden presence of this tree that I half expected it to shout, "Surprise!" Before inspecting it further, I glanced about, as if I had just done something mildly shameful, flinching before this new oak tree. But only a few souls were around this late in the semester, and they didn't seem much interested in me, or the tree.

The university groundskeepers had done a nice job planting our new oak, carving out a broad well at the base roughly six feet in diameter, which would ensure the efficient delivery of water and nutrients to the transplanted roots. It was a good spot along the quad, too, unshaded by the nearby, but not too nearby, banyan tree and palms. Plenty of room for the oak to gather sunlight and rain and do its thing. It was a beautiful specimen, already twelve feet tall or so, generously leafed out in its spring clothes, its trunk thick and straight for five feet before branching into several well-muscled arms. Someone who knew what he or she was doing had likely "trained" this tree over its first eight years or so to curb its sprawling proclivities, pruning those low, horizontally-inclined branches to encourage its more upright trajectory.

I stood there for several moments, taking in this new live oak in Florida. It seemed . . . remarkable, I suppose, that this new tree was suddenly here, occupying full-time this patch of ground at the center of my college campus that mere hours ago had been unoccupied. Strange, somehow, that the university waited until the semester was nearly over, the campus depleted, before planting the tree, and with no fanfare whatsoever. No ceremony or plaque or decorative ribbon-border. I'm not sure exactly what I had in mind for the tree as a more fitting welcome, but it seemed vaguely "off" that a particularly fine oak was in our midst without any to-do. Perhaps that's why I had reflexively surveyed the quad for other people upon spotting the oak. Not so much out of self-consciousness, but to share the discovery with anyone who happened to be around, as if it were a strange and wondrous and fleeting Florida sight, a rainbow, say, or a space-shuttle launch.

Why shouldn't a fine tree inspire equal wonder?

I decide that it will be worthwhile to know live oak better. Turns out there's a lot to learn. *Quercus virginiana.* Live oak. Also known as Virginia oak, southern live oak, sand live oak, scrub live oak, and Texas live oak. Its precise taxonomic status, uncertain. Some scientists recognize three distinct species, while others recognize mere varieties. A large spreading tree of the Coastal Plain ranging from southeastern Virginia to southern Florida, including the Florida Keys, and westward to the east end of the Brazos River in southern Texas. Live oak inhabits a wide variety of sites: pure stands, scrublands, hammocks, salt marshes, pastures, and mixed woodlands of laurel oak, sweetgum, southern magnolia, palms, laurel, bay, American holly, etc. Northern sensibilities, vis-à-vis the oak tree, will judge the leaves unusually small, un-oakishly small, two to five inches long by a half-inch to two-and-a-half inches wide, or thereabouts. Amorphously, unoakishly shaped, too. "The narrowly to broadly elliptical shaped leaves are usually stiff and leathery," the Forest Trees of Florida website suggests. "The upper surface is shiny, dark green. The leaves are dull grayish green underneath. The leaf base is tapering and the tip is short pointed to rounded. The margin is smooth and slightly wavy." It's unclear whether the live oak earned its common name because it retains most of its leaves throughout winter, when most other oaks have dropped their clothes, or because the tree hosts a variety of additional "live" flora across its roughly ridged bark—epiphytes, specifically, such as mistletoe (*Phoradendron*), ball moss, and Spanish moss (*Tillandsia usneoides*)—or whether both characteristics account for its name.

William Bartram, who offered the English-speaking world the first comprehensive botanical and zoological survey of the Carolinas, Georgia, and

Florida, was blessed with a sense of wonder for the natural phenomena he encountered on his perilous journey. Bartram's response to the prolific live oaks he encountered throughout his travels exemplifies his gift. He was unabashedly amazed by these trees. References to "majestic," "venerable," and "great" live oak stands permeate Bartram's *Travels* (1791), a book that did much to wrest the unconstructed realm of nature from prevailing Puritan notions of hostile wilderness, setting the stage for the Transcendentalists Emerson and Thoreau. A live oak offers Bartram welcome shade along the Altamaha River during one of the book's most reverential moments in nature. "My barque being securely moored, and having reconnoitered the surrounding groves, and collected fire-wood," Bartram writes, "I spread my skins and blanket by my chearful fire, under the protecting shade of the hospitable Live-oak, and reclined my head on my hard but healthy couch. I listened, undisturbed, to the divine hymns of the feathered songsters of the groves, whilst the softly whispering breezes faintly died away." It's this sense of wonder, above all, that courses through every page of Bartram's classic work.

Detached irony, by contrast, seems to be our default mode of experiencing the world, and writing about it. I, myself, have absorbed a fair measure of this contemporary sensibility. I can be quick to deploy a sarcastic quip or ironic gesture. But as I grow older I find myself striving, increasingly, to resist this impulse, which is mostly a defensive impulse. At least for me, I think. Irony is my way, I fear, of deflecting the emotions that experience inspires (such as wonder) rather than engaging foursquare with these emotions. I'd like to experience live oaks on their own terms as sincerely and straightforwardly, and unsarcastically, as Bartram did.

I'm in good company, to be sure. Marjory Stoneman Douglas might have had Bartram's account in mind while writing her own ecstatic description of live oaks in *The Everglades: River of Grass* (1947), the "first of the hardwoods" that displaced pines and palmettos in the wake of wildfires to form hammocks all about the 'glades. "The warblers in their thousands," Douglas writes, "migrate up and down the continents, spring and fall, South America to North America and back, enlivening the oaks with their small flitting shapes and tiny whisperings."

The story of live oaks and us, I discover, is more complex than I could have imagined. Live oaks harvested from Florida long served more utilitarian purposes than Bartram, or Douglas, would have appreciated. They proved themselves especially useful to the U.S. shipbuilding industry during the era of wooden ships, so useful that the U.S. Navy maintained its own live oak forests. A large stand of live oak planted by the U.S. Navy near Pensacola, Florida, was our first U.S. Government Forest. Lines of cells, called rays, run at convenient right angles to a live oak's growth rings, facilitating straight and true splits. The naval frigate USS *Constitution* (aka "Old Ironsides"), which famously deflected British cannon balls during the War of 1812, was built mostly from live oak of the Georgia sea islands and New England white oak, roughly 1,500 oaks in all. The gentle curves of sloping live oak branches were particularly well suited to a ship hull's curved knee braces.

Live oak wood now serves few commercial purposes.

White and black settlements in Florida would increasingly crop up during the nineteenth century in the wake of Bartram's journey. Roughly one hundred years after he left Florida for good, the new state was just hospitable enough for another writer, Harriet Beecher Stowe, to not only visit but also take up a winter residence along the St. John's river in Mandarin, near St. Augustine. A great live oak, festooned with Spanish moss, canopied the Stowes' front porch, purportedly the most photographed front porch in the community. Stowe had published her wildly successful *Uncle Tom's Cabin* (1852) some fifteen years before taking up her winter residence in Mandarin, and her publisher was anxious for her to produce another novel cut from similar, fashionable literary cloth. In an act of artistic bravery, she produced *Palmetto-Leaves* (1873) instead, an interconnected series of sketches on northern Florida's unique botanical riches, pitched explicitly to enlighten a readership blinded by northeastern environmental sensibilities. While she named her book after the ubiquitous palmetto, her awestruck description of the live oak—which she first sees in Savannah, Georgia, before arriving at Florida's border—precedes her account of the palmetto. "How shall we give a person who has never seen live-oaks or gray moss an idea of it?" she worries.

I didn't know anything about live oaks—or that Harriet Beecher Stowe wrote an environmental nonfiction narrative called *Palmetto-Leaves*—when I moved to south Florida in 1996. I didn't even know that these sprawling, muscular trees were oaks, given their small leaves. But I did notice and admire them. The two enormous specimens on our neighbor's property, which canopy our own backyard under their protective shade, sealed our decision to buy our house. As our affable real-estate agent nattered on about school districts, resale values, and square footage under air, we were transfixed by those heirloom oaks dappling the chattahoochee patio with their shadow fingerprints. The house is lucky to have these big oaks to brook the heat; it's fairly unusual to enjoy such old trees as neighbors in Boca Raton developments. Most of the neighborhoods are fairly new along our stretch of the coastal ridge between the Everglades and the ocean. Our 1981 home is considered "old" construction, a vaguely shameful designation that undermines its value, not unlike a car with over 100,000 miles on the odometer. Florida, increasingly, is a state that celebrates the new and that exhibits little tolerance for what it deems old, including its flora. Refusing to conform to the space-crunching grids of suburban developers, most of the native oaks, palms, mahogany, slash pine, and gumbo limbo in my subdivision were simply cleared away, fast-growing arboreal imposters such as olive, ficus, and Australian pine—all problematic for various reasons—plopped down in less obtrusive locales.

While chambers of commerce and real-estate developers throughout Florida continue to promote their version of "progress," the countervailing impulse to promote and preserve "old" Florida's natural beauty sometimes holds sway. My own town, for example, ranks currently as one of Florida's 129 Tree City USA communities, one of only 5 Tree Cities in the state to have maintained its designation for at least 27 years. Tree Cities are certified by the Division of Forestry in Florida and the Arbor Day Foundation, which means that my community and other Florida Tree Cities maintain the following four criteria: 1) a Tree Board or Department, 2) a Tree Care Ordinance, 3) a Community Forestry Program with an annual budget of at least $2 per capita, and 4) an Arbor Day Observance Proclamation. To celebrate Arbor Day in 2008, Governor Charlie Crist and the Florida Department of Environmental Protection encouraged all Florida citizens to plant native trees to offset the potential impact of climate change. Like many other Tree Cities throughout Florida—from Altamonte Springs to Zephyrhills—my city helps to make this possible as Arbor Day comes around each year by selling a varying assortment of native Florida trees to its residents at discounted rates. My wife and I have planted two live oaks on our property through this program. Our city also undertakes various other tree-planting initiatives in cooperation with local elementary schools to celebrate Arbor Day. This usually goes pretty well, although there was an embarrassing episode in the early 1980s when the live oak planted next to City Hall withered and died shortly thereafter.

While it's great to plant new trees, our oldest, biggest trees are the ones over which we rightly marvel. An archival photograph at my town's historical society features three sandy-haired children at play beneath the gnarled, horizontal branches of a live oak festooned with bromeliad and Spanish moss. A grove of gnarled live oaks looms in the blurry background behind a short plaster wall. The girls' short-cropped hair, which frames their round faces, betrays the south Florida heat, or perhaps only the fashion, circa 1910. The barefooted boy crouches on all fours before his metal toy car. He stares directly at the camera, unsmiling. A dog pants on its haunches in the foreground, the live oak canopy providing only limited relief from the sun's heat, maybe.

The Treaty Oak in Austin, Texas, is probably the most famous live oak in the country. Estimated by forestry experts to be about five hundred years old, the Treaty Oak is the only oak of the original fourteen Council Oaks in the once-grove to survive development and neglect. Comanche and Tonkawa Indians joined under its canopy to hold sacred meetings. Women of the Tejas tribe drank tea made from the tree's acorns to ensure the safety of their warrior men during battle. Additional legends abound. A vandal, stung by unrequited love, poisoned the mighty oak in 1989, prompting international news coverage and thousands of get-well letters (to the tree, not to the vandal) from bereft schoolchildren. Ross Perot wrote a blank check to facilitate the Treaty Oak's care and recovery. The live oak survived, about 35 percent of it, anyway. Eight years after its poisoning, the lopsided tree produced a new crop of acorns.

There's a fairly old "Treaty Oak" in Jacksonville, Florida, too, this one something of a fraud. To preclude its axing by developers, a local journalist in the 1930s issued specious claims involving vague historic treaties and Native Americans in an article featured in the *Florida Times-Union*. The ruse worked. The tree lives. Online, you can purchase "Treaty Oak" postcards of the Jacksonville specimen.

Closer to my home, the "Council Oak Tree" at Stirling Road and State Road 7 in Hollywood, Florida, is where members of the Seminole tribe have met for years. No hoax here. Surrounded now by urban sprawl, including one of the tribe's bustling casinos, it started out as a shady spot that could accommodate large numbers of attendees in the years before air conditioning. The tribe recently nominated the impressive specimen for inclusion in the National Register of Historic Places.

The largest surviving Florida live oak stands near Gainesville, in Alachua County, and measures 30 feet in circumference and 85 feet in height, with a 160-foot spread. Florida's state tree isn't the live oak but the Cabbage palmetto, which I suppose I can get behind as Georgia beat Florida to the punch, claiming the live oak as their state tree.

There is a Live Oak, Florida, a Live Oak, Texas, and a Live Oak, California. The towns seem principally to tout their proximity to other, better places. "Gateway to San Antonio," the Live Oak, Texas, homepage declares. The California burg's website boasts, "It is strategically located along the Highway 99 corridor between Yuba City and Chico, and has easy access to San Francisco, Lake Tahoe, and Sacramento." The city of Live Oak, Florida, proximate to the famous Suwannee River, claims to be within short driving distance to four, curiously undisclosed, large metropolitan areas. The shopping center just down the street from my subdivision is called the Live Oak Plaza. The conference center on my college campus is called the Live Oak Pavilion. My kids will attend Camp Live Oak this summer.

We don't know exactly how to feel about live oaks, it seems to me the more that I learn. The plot of land that my university now occupies exemplifies our longstanding ambivalent, even tortured, relationship with trees, generally. Originally a scrubland of slash pine, wax myrtle, saw palmetto, cabbage palmetto, and live oak, the land was mostly cleared early in the twentieth century—the trees grubbed out, stumps and all, sometimes with dynamite—to make way for agriculture. A local airport and a World War II Army air field supplanted the farmland, pretty much leveling whatever trees remained in the area. Then, in the 1960s, the university supplanted the defunct Army air field and devoted its scant resources primarily to propping up academic and administrative buildings. The upshot: there weren't too many trees at all on my college campus, even as late as my arrival in the mid-1990s. Bartram and Stowe would have been aghast at the look of the place.

Then, suddenly, we enjoyed a windfall of new trees. "Three separate donations from a Miami tree farm between 1998 and 2000, or thereabouts," the operations manager at my university grounds department tells me over the phone. Practically overnight, the campus was transformed from a vacated warren of bleak, squat, 1970s-style architecture to a leafy expanse of still-bleak, still-squat, 1970s-style architecture. We're now all about the trees, it would appear, but only insofar as those trees don't interfere with other, more privileged, pursuits. Our new, ironically "green," building for the College of Nursing was erected a few years ago right on top of one of the loveliest live oak groves on campus. A few years before the nursing building supplanted the old trees, the university erected a strip mall on its land just west of the main campus, clearing one of the few remaining oak scrub buffers in town for the likes of Bed Bath & Beyond, Whole Foods, and Barnes & Noble. Our new football stadium and "Innovation Village"—replete with dormitories, restaurants, and shops—have squeezed out countless live oaks and associated flora and fauna at the formerly undeveloped northern end of my campus. Our cheer—"Go Owls!"—now contains an unfortunate double entendre. I suppose it's for these reasons that I've always cast a jaundiced eye toward our university's priorities, vis-à-vis its landscape.

Yet, some grand old live oaks have survived on my campus, and, like grand old humans, they have a story. A former chair of the math department, I discover, led an effort in the 1970s to rescue several live oaks from the obliterating path of the I-95 construction project, rapidly heading southward. His goal was to transplant them onto FAU's campus. Jack Freeman. I know this fellow, vaguely. He's a short and scraggly codger who rides an equally dilapidated bicycle around campus. The officially retired Freeman still teaches math as an adjunct and exercises at the university fitness center, where I was once introduced to him. "We were very ambitious," he tells me now over the phone. "We moved upwards of 500, 600 trees or so. Mostly big ones. The whole thing took us two and a half, three years." I'm disappointed, though unsurprised, to learn from Jack that our university administration "raised all kinds of objections from the get go" and "didn't care at all about native trees." So Jack sent a letter to Governor Reubin Askew and his entire cabinet. "They, on the other hand, loved the idea," he tells me. "Once Tallahassee put the squeeze on the administration, they had to help, or at least not interfere." Jack pauses here over the phone line and I can hear him start to laugh, faintly. "The administration really hated my guts then," he recalls, chortling at the memory. For the next half hour or so, Jack, a native Floridian who clearly knows a great deal about trees, describes the three-step root-prune process they used to transplant the large live oaks: "You have to make a clean cut at the roots, then cover it back up, come back two or three months later, hopefully you get a lot of rain in the meantime, then do it again, wait another two or three months if you have the time. That's the best way to encourage the hair roots." I ask Jack what kinds of tools he had at his disposal for such big trees, such heavy work. He tells me that the equipment came from a variety of sources. Tallahassee ordered the Department of Transportation to lend his group a combination backhoe and front-end loader, along with a licensed operator; the National Audubon Society gave them some money to pay for the giant crane owned by the Boynton Landscape Company, "the largest crane in the state at the time," Jack recalls. The Division of Forestry donated some equipment, too, and cash donations came in from a variety of sources. I tell Jack that I'm interested in knowing which live oaks on campus were his live oaks, the ones he and a handful of colleagues had transplanted. "Well," he asks, "do you want to take a walk?"

We meet on campus the following week and Jack leads me through the campus grounds, pointing out "project oaks" all about. Jack walks slowly, and stooped, not unlike a lumbering bear. It's a sweltering June day, and I soon feel somewhat guilty for accepting this tour of the campus. But Jack, though he moves slowly, seems unperturbed by the heat (whereas I'm feeling vaguely nauseated). After a half hour or so, it becomes clear that any oak of a certain size is probably one of Jack's trees. "You can also tell which ones the university planted," he explains, pointing derisively toward a few young trees, "because they plop them down in straight rows." Taking in all these giant oaks, mostly live oaks, but several laurel oaks, as well, it seems to me that Jack should be mighty pleased with his efforts. Yet he spends just as much time on our walk pointing out the ghosts of his live oaks, the once-trees having been bulldozed to make room for the Student Services Building, the extension to the University Center, the ironically named Live Oak Pavilion, the library parking lot. And so I ask him directly how it feels to walk around the campus now, whether it pleases or depresses him. "I usually walk through with blinders on," he answers. A few strides later, he points toward a sidewalk and remarks, "They 'dozed a big old oak because it was in their way. I told them, 'Where I come from, we build a sidewalk *around* a tree like that.'" Despite it all, I'm pleased to observe that Jack still has a good bit of spunk left in him. When I complain about the messiness of the non-native olive trees about, he gently chides me, "I forgive trees for being messy. They're supposed to drop their leaves and such."

Funny, live oaks and us. We bulldoze the most impressive specimens to make way for buildings; we rescue and transplant them; we poison them with picloram at two and four pounds per acre to maximize grassland pasture for insatiable cattle; we poison them to lament unrequited love; children send them get-well cards; we grub them out for farmland; we erect monuments underneath their shade; we feature them in novels and films; we conscript them to help us carry out unspeakable racial atrocities. Southern trees bear strange fruit, as Billie Holiday sang.

Not to say that my own experience with live oaks has been uncomplicated. I like to think that I've done okay by the trees, on the whole. The two fine specimens I bought and planted on my property during my city's Arbor Day drives are coming along nicely. We snap a photograph of Henry and Sophia posing before the larger tree, as parents do, on the first day of school each year, marking the growth of both our tree and our kids.

All the same, I'm not above whacking down a live oak sprig on my property when it gets in my way. Curiously, one such sprig in my yard has managed to foil my eradication efforts. It volunteered a few years ago right smack in the middle of our elevated vegetable bed, between the eggplant and okra leaves. Hidden within the floppy foliage, it was a foot high or so before I noticed it. Without a suitable tool on hand, I tugged at it a few times, but it wouldn't budge. It was really in there. For whatever reason, I let it go for a while longer, not really noticing the sprig again until it had grown another foot or so and sprouted new tender leaves. This wouldn't do, a shade tree growing in our vegetable garden. I happened to have been wielding a handheld tree-limb saw this time, so I held the sapling taut and took a couple haphazard swipes at it. Again, it stood its ground and I somehow didn't have the heart to force the issue. This pattern repeated itself a few more times before the live oak sprig caught the attention of my wife and son, both of whom convinced me to leave the poor thing alone. The tree is now taller than I am. While it still may not be much to look at, by live oak standards, I regard it now with something close to awe. That it managed to fend off my frequent—albeit half-assed—attacks. The moxie! It'll have to go soon, but we won't be walking it to the curb for large debris pickup. We'll transplant the live oak, instead. A neighbor has already called dibs. Meanwhile, I've come to view my eradication efforts as emblematic of our collective, fraught relationship with live oaks, with trees, and with the unconstructed natural realm, generally.

That largest live oak in Florida, near Gainesville, isn't too far from the sleepover gardening camp that my son will attend for a week this summer; neither is Marjorie Kinnan Rawlings' house and environs in Cross Creek, which inspired her Florida novels and her memoir, *Cross Creek* (1942). And so we decide to drop in on the oak, and the Marjorie Kinnan Rawlings' Historic State Park, before dropping off Henry. He's not much of a talker, our son, so we figure that the trip might offer him a conversation piece with his new friends and that these kids who've voluntarily decided to attend a gardening sleepover camp might actually care to hear something about Florida's largest live oak and Rawlings' property. We traverse, somewhat ironically, that oak-decimating I-95 for part of the trip before joining up with the Florida Turnpike and then I-75, which takes us beyond the mobbed exits of Orlando's Disney World up toward the woolly northern middle of the state, toward Cellon Oak Park in Alachua County. Off the interstate, finally, it's beautiful horse country along a series of small highways, green rolling hills with stands of large oak and pine, which don't typically get the chance to grow so big in my more constructed part of the state. We're very good at planting trees in my town and at my university, this trip makes me realize; we're just not very good at respecting their occupancy.

Even though Cellon Oak Park is quite close to a big university town, it's not at all easy to find. My wife and I squabble over our predicament as we meander along Route 121, which I'm fairly certain will lead us there. She can't fathom why I didn't get specific directions off the Internet. By the time we got this close, I explain, I figured that there would be signs along the road. But there aren't any signs for the park. It's the largest live oak in the state! It must receive some visitors. As we proceed uncertainly along the highway, I worry that there might be something self-indulgent about this whole trip. What will we do, anyway, once we lay eyes on the tree? Turn right around to stay at our overnight lodgings?

Finally, we see a single, small brown sign for the park directing us to turn left. A small dirt road takes us to a large clearing of well-shorn grass, and there it is! The Cellon Oak. We're the only ones here. We see the tree looming before us some hundred yards away, dripping with Spanish moss. It still looks healthy and proud, I'm happy to see, some limbs growing along the ground, per the live oak's predilections, but a high canopy too with plenty of young, light-green leaves. "That's quite a tree," I say, which is a stupid thing to say, maybe, but what else is there to say? A new-looking metal sign at the entrance reads,

Florida Champion Tree
Live Oak
Height 79 Feet
Circumference 344"/29 Feet
Average Crown Spread 154 Feet

These are smaller dimensions than I've seen claimed for this tree elsewhere. It's raining, but we all get out of the car anyway with a couple small umbrellas and head toward the oak. I click off a few photos, then hide my camera from the rain underneath my tee shirt. As if on cue, the rain subsides as we near and the sky brightens some. The only thing missing is a rainbow. Our kids run out from underneath the umbrellas and race toward the trunk. An older plaque, from 1987, stands on a wooden post before the tree, and I notice that the dimensions are the same as those on the newer sign. Surely, this robust tree must have grown some over the past twenty-two years. For whatever reason, they just didn't update the newer sign. My son, a tree-climber, pats the behemoth trunk and makes a funny gesture with his leg, pretending to begin his ascent. I pat the gnarly trunk too. There's something about patting a big old tree like this. You can feel its heft and age. My wife and I take in the tree. We notice, especially, the enormous branch that shoots at a diagonal from the trunk some ten feet off the ground. Wendy, ever the skeptic, wonders how they know that it's a single tree, and not two or three live oaks that had grown together. I don't have an answer for this.

"You can climb up on that branch maybe," I say to Henry and Sophia, pointing to an enormous downward-stretching limb that lay on the ground some fifty feet from the base. They clamber up the huge branch together and I click off a few more photos. Someone a long time ago had tried to lift this limb, it seems, because a steel cable stretches up into the enormous canopy from a large rivet, which the oak branch has nearly consumed. (I'll learn later that the steel cable is part of a lightning rod.) My wife and I lay our hands on the branch. The bark on its topmost section, exposed to the elements over the past five hundred years or so, is smooth, Wendy notices, whereas the bark underneath is rough.

I had worried that we wouldn't have much to do at the park, that it would seem, in short, a stupid trip to my kids. But we all find plenty to entertain ourselves with. My son and daughter collect Spanish moss on the ground and tie the clusters around their faces, making big beards. A flock of chickadees wheeze high up in the canopy, and some eastern blue birds flit about on nearby telephone lines. We don't have chickadees or blue birds in Boca Raton, and so we enjoy the treat of watching them for a while. There are several other fine trees in this field, some live oaks and others I can't identify, so we make the rounds inspecting all the trees. Sophia tries in vain to locate a woodpecker she hears up in the branches of one tree. We all join her, but none of us can find the darn bird. "Maybe it's inside its hole," she says, and she's probably right. Sophia and Henry proceed to play hide-and-go-seek, and any number of variations, around the enormous live oak and among the other big trees. We stay for a couple hours or so, until the kids deplete themselves. Again, there's plenty to do beneath the canopy of a big old tree.

We spend the night nearby and make our way to Cross Creek and Rawlings' home the next morning, before taking Henry to his camp. An affable fifty-something fellow in bare feet gives us a tour of the house. He's a local, it turns out, whose family knew Rawlings quite well. She stitched clothes for his father and his aunt to encourage them to attend school, but they stuck it out only long enough to lay claim to the clothes, he tells us. The house, itself, is quite large. The old pine flooring creaks under our weight as we travel room to room. It strikes me as a hallowed place to see the patio where Rawlings sometimes slept to brook the heat, her old Singer sewing machine, the wooden cupboard where she hid her alcohol during prohibition, the salad bowl she jerry-rigged for a light fixture, the dated linoleum and kitchen appliances. My daughter, however, finds the house "creepy."

Our guide makes special mention of the citrus trees that they maintain all about the property, because Rawlings maintained an even larger citrus grove. He encourages us on several occasions to come back in the winter, when we can harvest and keep the oranges. But, of course, it's the larger oaks all about the property, water oaks and live oaks, that mostly appeal to me—the tall sabal palms and the enormous magnolia tree near the barn, too, a tree that Rawlings wrote about, specifically. The citrus trees are all young and transplanted, after all, whereas these enormous oaks, palms, and the magnolia are the very same trees that Rawlings herself gazed upon and tended when she lived here. It's hot and buggy, but my family and I spend some time tracking three pileated woodpeckers from tree to tree, as Rawlings surely spent some time doing too some fifty-odd years ago. Besides her writing, it seems to me the most tangible connection we share with Rawlings, glimpsing these same trees and their affiliated creatures. The connection is more tangible and real to me, somehow, than glimpsing her bathtub and bed. Sophia's right, I contemplate on the way back to the car. There is something creepy about seeing someone's home—the most intimate furnishings of one's daily life—turned into a museum, while it's not creepy at all to gaze upon Rawlings' trees.

Back on my university campus the next week, I notice that our splendid new live oak tree has been granted its own plaque, after all. I see the damp, rectangular cement base one day; the next day, a small, roughhewn, faux-granite marker appears with a small plaque, affixed. A quotation from Dr. Seuss's environmental classic, *The Lorax* (1971), takes up most of the space: "Unless someone like you cares a whole awful lot, nothing is going to get better. It's not." The inscription below suggests that the tree has been donated by our student environmental association, FAU Mission Green, on Earth Day, April 22, 2009.

In an ideal world, or at least my halcyon notion of such a world, trees would be so prevalent that it would seem silly to erect a plaque to announce any single specimen. Moreover, there would be so many five-hundred-year-old live oaks that determining the single largest tree among these manifold giants would also seem silly, if not impossible. That we require plaques for our new trees, and our especially old ones, betrays their embattlement and general diminution in our postindustrial age. But this *is* the age we live in; and this *is* the state of the live oaks and their cousins. And so I'm happy to see this plaque before this lovely, young live oak, happy too that it hasn't been planted to honor a person but to honor itself, for all intents and purposes. A live oak planted to celebrate the singular, splendid phenomenon of live oakness in this world.

3

Coontie

KIDS CAN BREAK YOUR HEART. Henry, his gaze fixed upon the blight, was devastated. Just the day before, everything looked fine at our neighborhood park, a relatively new park replete with top-of-the-line swing sets, slides, and climbing apparatuses beneath a live oak canopy. But at some point over the last twenty-four hours, without any warning whatsoever, the hundred or so low-lying coontie plants, which had circled the play area like wagons, had vanished. I followed my son closer to the scene of the crime and watched him as he looked straight down at a bare patch of soil that had just yesterday supported the vaguely prehistoric tendrils of one of the coontie plants.

"Where'd they all go?" he finally asked, his thick brows forming their familiar worried furrow.

"Don't worry, we'll call someone," I answered, lamely, as if a phone call would set matters aright.

Coontie. Scientific name: *Zamia pumila*. Or *Zamia integrifolia*. Or *Zamia umbrosa*. Or *Zamia floridana*. Linnaeus, in 1763, attributed the origins of *Zamia pumila* to Cuba, Puerto Rico, and the Dominican Republic, and taxonomists continue to debate whether Florida *Zamia*—distributed across a variety of well-drained, sandy-soil habitats throughout the peninsula—constitutes a distinct species, or even two distinct species. In any case, the coontie plant is a relatively small, shrub-like perennial, its narrow spiky leaflets of four to six inches forming the drooping, dark-green leaves of three feet or so. Individual coontie plants boast male or female reproductive cones, rendering them dioecious. These rusty cones burst straight up from the ground at the center of the plant in late winter. The untrained eye could mistake the plant for a type of palm or fern. Coonties, however, belong to the separate order of Cycads, which dates back to the early Permian period. During the dinosaur era, Cycads reigned supreme in the plant world, making them living fossils today!

What's more, coontie plants serve as the only known host plant for the atala butterfly (*Eumaeus atala*), a small, black butterfly accented with iridescent blue wing-specks and scarlet abdomens. A natural toxin in the coontie leaves protects the vulnerable atala larvae from predators. Atalas lucky enough to reach the adult stage exhibit a low and erratic flight pattern; a crash seems imminent at any moment. Males and females court and mate in the late afternoon, and the females deposit up to forty eggs on coontie leaves, singly or in clusters. Then, within ten days of emerging from their pupas, the atalas expire.

Coontie plants support humans, as well. Calusa, Timucua, and, later, Seminole Native Americans harvested the plant's large storage root and extracted the edible starch to make bread. The name "coontie" in fact, means "flour root," "white root," or "bread" in the Seminole language. White settlers called the plant "arrowroot" and harvested them to make the popular arrowroot biscuits. By the 1900s, several industrial factories had cropped up in south Florida, some of them processing up to fifteen tons of "arrowroot" powder per day. Individual coontie plants, however, grow slowly. The upshot: by 1965, only isolated patches of wild coontie plants could be found in Florida and the atala butterfly was thought to be extinct.

The park employee at the city claimed that the city had removed the coontie plants because they were overgrown and unhealthy. He surprised me by being ready, apparently, to answer my next concern—what would happen to all the atala butterflies that the plants had supported? He suggested that the butterfly clouds actually encouraged lustier predation by birds, lizards, rats, what have you, and was bad for the overall atala population.

"That doesn't make any sense!" Henry said after I recounted the park employee's explanation. My son took the loss of our neighborhood coontie plants hard because we had just learned about them a few months ago. We had noticed the strange black-blue-red butterflies aflutter above the plants, inspected the narrow leaves, and spied the rust-colored pupa (disguised as withering leaves) and even a few of the burnt-orange caterpillars, accented with florescent yellow dots—a whole life cycle on display. We knew that the plants had to be special. And so we learned about the coontie's ancient origins, its atala butterflies, its starchy prize beneath the soil. How could our town grub out such a robust population of the coontie, a population that they were smart enough to plant when they opened the park just a few years earlier? They had uprooted them, it seemed clear, because the plants were deemed sloppy, and sloppy is one trait that my town simply doesn't tolerate in its flora.

Henry would not be appeased. "If they just would have told us," he complained, "we would have taken them to *our* house." Yes, it was a shame. But we could still find and plant a few coonties, I assured him, the thought just then dawning in my mind. This seemed to sit well with Henry. It wasn't easy finding coontie plants for sale, and we were forced to pay an exorbitant price when we finally did locate a listless patch at a local butterfly exhibit. We planted on our property five small coonties that, true to their inclinations, have grown at an impossibly slow pace. Yet they continue on, doggedly, now and again advertising new, paler-green foliage. But mostly they look the same.

I had hoped for larger, lustier plants by now. Here in Florida, plants tend to grow rather quickly, almost bizarrely so. We enjoy a twelve-month growing season, after all. Flora here is blessed with ample light and heat and water. It's all I can do to keep up with my trimming of the randy firebush beside our five coonties to prevent the shrub from shrouding its smaller neighbors. Yet there's something especially poignant about our few small coonties. The slow growth rate of the plants makes me marvel all the more at their prehistoric bona fides. Since the early Permian period, multiple millennia earlier than us hominids emerged, coonties have been doing their thing and doing it well, parsing their energies deliberately between cone and seed and shoot. That we had nearly wiped out coonties in Florida by the 1960s illustrates, frighteningly, how quickly the rise of postindustrial humankind has upset the organic order on Earth.

With this in mind, I take especially careful stock of these Cycads, these living fossils, each day in the garden. There's something magical about the new growth they push out at the center, those humble pale-green fronds that seem to emerge out of nowhere when I must not have been paying attention and then over weeks, months, uncurl slowly, oh so slowly, like the fingers of a small hand. But who am I to call all this "slow"? Who am I to impose my human notions of time on these timeless specimens?

It's been a few years and we still haven't seen any atala butterflies in our yard. This may be a good thing, as a robust population of the creatures would surely decimate our humble plants. Henry, however, would like to see the butterflies sooner rather than later. "Too bad we can't just put a sign out for them," he joked a while back. His sense of time, like mine, is decidedly human, by which I mean impatient. We would do well to adjust our internal clocks closer to coontie-time. "They'll come," I assured him. "Any day now. Patience."

4

Fishing in the Dark

I'VE LIVED ALONG THE COAST of Florida for several years now. It's high time I learn how to fish. It's something of an embarrassment, really, living on a peninsula surrounded by water, one that lifts its toe above rich piscatorial waters, and experiencing so little of it. My immersions in Florida's aquatic realm have been tentative and timid up until now. I eat local fish that I buy at the fishmonger. I visit the beach with my family from time to time, paddle about in the shallows and snorkel a bit, gaze at the mangrove snapper schools holding fast in the current against one of our shallow, man-made reefs. How do they get from this reef, to the fishmonger, to my plate? I find myself craving deeper contact. As I venture just beyond the sandbar, treading water, I lift my chin above the waterline and look eastward, out to sea, tracing with my eyes the progress of vessels offshore that make their way to and from various destinations utterly foreign to me. I watch until the vessels disappear. These people know something about this place that I don't know. I, too, yearn to leave the shore behind. But I'll need a teacher.

"I only fish at night," he warns. "Grew up in Minnesota. Can't handle the sun. Fishing's better at night, anyway."

"Oh, okay," I reply, because what else can I say? A colleague from political science, Tim's the only person I know who owns a boat. It just never occurred to me that people who owned boats would take them out to sea at night. *Fishing Capital of the World!* the television advertisements boast in hopes of luring ever more tourists to our financially strapped state. It's always daytime in these ads. Giant tarpon leap silver above the cerulean waters of a Keys flat, sailfish in the open Atlantic skitter across the frame behind behemoth Sportfisher vessels, a defeated yellowtail snapper dangles from the line of a happier, sandy-haired child squinting into the sun.

That's sort of what I have in mind. The fantastical version of Florida, marketed shrewdly to prospective tourists and in-state "stay-cationers" alike. But out in the middle of the choppy Atlantic during blackest night? A nineteen-foot length of molded fiberglass and a single gas engine between me and the unforgiving sea? Am I ready to experience the real Florida, unmediated by the lights, camera, action of a professional television crew?

Truth is, I'm afraid.

On my way to the ramp, I pass the darkened storefronts of private galleries and upscale restaurants on our busiest downtown street. It's not late, but our little burg along Florida's southeastern Gold Coast goes to sleep impossibly early. Instead of the usual street noise, I can hear through my open car window the wind breathing through the stiff date palm fronds. The boat-launch park just off this normally busy street is eerily quiet, too. My brakes groan as I pull up to a spot facing the black intracoastal waterway. I've visited the ramp countless times during the day to check out the boats. It's raucous here during daylight hours. On a typical weekend day I'll see boats and aluminum trailers lined up ten deep in two separate lanes to launch and retrieve. Hopped-up college kids wearing low-slung swim trunks and the sparsest bikinis regale one another after disembarking at the dock; younger kids and their parents futilely wet their lines there between the parked vessels; pot-bellied fishermen run freshwater through their engines at the wash-down. Tempers flare at the concrete ramp over perceived infractions against launching or retrieval protocol. Angry tirades erupt accompanied by the growl of overpowered engines passing up and down the congested waterway.

But it's nighttime now, and the place is entirely strange to me. No line at the ramp. No hopped-up teenagers or weekend warriors. Only the long aluminum skeletons of a few parked trailers. A black man in a white undershirt sits at the boatless dock, his fishing line lowered into the syrupy water. A leaner white man with a scruffy beard shuffles about the parking lot, exuding a vague air of homelessness. A feral cat herd, having gathered courage, mobs the fragrant trash can over-brimming now with depleted cardboard sardine boxes and dented cans of cheap pilsner. A bladder of melted ice quivers on the concrete below.

"Well, ready?" my friend asks, hands on his hips. Over his chest, a silver nail-clipper for cutting fishing line hangs from a shoelace. He wears a broad fishing hat, as if he doesn't realize that the sun tucked itself in hours ago. I tell him "sure," and he tells me to stand on the dock beside the ramp so he can launch the boat. He dips the trailer in the drink and shouts out the window for me to grab the blue rope on his deck. Then, he backs the trailer more aggressively, pops his truck into Drive, and sort of bucks the boat off its bunkers and into the water. *Don't drop the rope,* I warn myself.

"You don't wear a life jacket?" I ask as we motor slowly through the minimum wake intracoastal toward the inlet. I stand beside him at the console, gripping the aluminum frame of the boat's T-top.

"No," he says. "You want one?"

I fear I'll insult his captainship if I say yes, so I decline.

It's winter in Florida and pretty cold on the water, even here in the intracoastal waterway sheltered between the high shoulders of condos bejeweled with light. I'm glad that I brought a sweatshirt. Tim wears only a tattered button-down, long-sleeve shirt and doesn't seem cold. He's from Minnesota, I remind myself.

"How rough's it supposed to be out there tonight?" I ask as we reach the rock jetty of the inlet, leaving the brighter intracoastal behind. The only thing I can see now is the blinking red light up ahead to the left marking the north end of the inlet and the blinking green light to its right marking the south. The open ocean is right out there in front of us, I know, but it's impossibly dark—I can't find the moon anywhere—and I can't distinguish sky from sea.

"Shouldn't be too bad."

I don't find this comforting.

The bow rises above the first invisible wave at the inlet's mouth then dips low, along with my stomach. We plow northward slowly through the chop, the bow every so often slapping a wave with a *thwack* that doesn't sound good at all to my ears. I can tell that Tim wants to go faster because he keeps tapping the throttle forward but then pulls it back as soon as the bow slaps down too hard against the sea, throwing up a foamy torrent. Tim scans the Australian pine silhouettes on the faraway shoreline as we rise and dip, rise and dip, watching for his telltale marker of the reef deep below, I imagine. It strikes me as odd that he doesn't use a GPS. After motoring a while he says "okay" in a hopeful rising register and throws overboard from its rubber container a great steel claw of an anchor, which disappears immediately in the inky sea. Once the anchor sets, the stern swings to the north and the boat begins to buck more nervously against the chop. I train my eyes on the silhouettes of the Australian pines to keep from getting seasick as Tim rigs the rods, slips a frozen block of chum into a mesh bag, and begins slicing up stinky sardines for chunk-bait, tossing slivers off the stern in a broad fan as if he were spreading wildflower seeds. It's a dance of sorts that he performs on deck, but I don't know the steps. I want to do something to help, but it's all I can do to keep from throwing up. Finally, he hands me a rod baited with a thawed silverside minnow and after the briefest of instruction tells me to give it a shot.

There's not much to recommend the evening from a certain perspective. It's a long tiring night, as Tim had warned me in advance. The chop never wholly subsides so we struggle throughout the evening to maintain our balance. It's unmistakably dangerous. Commercial and recreational fishermen die fairly regularly off the coast of Florida after small acts of carelessness. I know this. Of recent note, two NFL players and a friend perished in 2009 after their twenty-one-foot fishing boat capsized in the Gulf of Mexico. (One person on board survived and was rescued by the Coast Guard after clinging to the overturned vessel for nearly two days.) Their mistake? When they couldn't free the stubborn anchor from the sea floor, they unwisely re-fastened the anchor-line from the bow to the stern and attempted to motor out, capsizing their vessel in the process.

Fishing for snapper is a dirty and smelly business, too. I wince especially when Tim lands a gleaming blue runner, a type of jack, and immediately carves up one side of the quivering, very-much-alive fish like a checkerboard for strip bait. There must be a better, more humane, way to do this, I think. And it's cold. My fingers, slimy with fish-ooze, tremble as I bait my hooks with slender silversides.

But mostly it's dark. A dusky overhead light on the T-top provides our only illumination. We labor for hours in the near black, bobbing like a teacup in the Atlantic, bracing ourselves against the gunwales as we squint against bird's nest tangles in our lines, as we grope blindly with pliers inside fishmouths for ingested hooks, as Tim struggles to identify and measure fish pulled from the sea.

"That's a glass eye . . . that's a mangrove snapper . . . that's a grunt . . . that's a squirrel fish, careful of the gill plates."

It seems to me that if I fished only at night, I'd trick out my boat with manifold lights, deck lights and spreaders out the back and front. I eventually ask Tim why he doesn't install more lights on his boat, and he references vague plans for the future, the complications of marine electronics. Yet, after struggling a while in the dark chop, it occurs to me that there's something . . . what's the word? . . . *true* about passing the time this way. The rare words we share on deck are soft words, soft as the dark. Tim lifts his finger skyward and identifies Orion's belt. I raise my eyes and see countless stars. I clear my throat, just to make certain that I'm there. And I wonder whether there's another reason Tim doesn't install more lights—because he knows that if he did so, he'd use them.

We savor the light. It's not for nothing that "Let there be Light" are the first words attributed to God in the Hebrew Bible. What good was a heaven and an earth if it was shrouded in darkness? But it is good sometimes, maybe, not to see with our eyes, and instead to court, in this way, disorientation, or at least a new orientation that might help us to find ourselves. The light and noise of my workaday life is only a quarter-mile away. Yet, bobbing on this dark ocean, it seems much farther away than that. What matters now is not whatever may be scheduled in my daily planner for the morning. What matters now isn't even the fish, really, tending to their own business along the reef, below. What matters now is only this perfect, simple knot that I'm trying with my trembling, slime-coated fingers to tie to the eye of this hook, my inhalations and exhalations, and the beating of my heart, which I can somehow feel in my throat.

Make no mistake. It feels uncommonly good to bounce in off the waves and slip inside the inlet to the placid intracoastal. The lights framing the old hotel seem to wink especially for us, welcoming us home.

"Pretty," Tim says.

"Yeah. Sure is."

We reach the ramp well after midnight, stinking of frozen bait and depleted, my abdominal muscles sore from beating back the chop, my hands stinging from the saltwater. But I know that I'll return if my fishing partner invites me. I've been offered a glimpse of the sea, a glimpse at what it takes to make the fish of the ocean the food on our plates. What I don't know is all that I'll experience out on the dark water over the next several years. I'll hear the human breath of loggerhead turtles above the dark skin of the sea and glimpse their broad caramel shells before they descend. I'll see the moon cast spears of light from between the clouds on faraway lapping swells. My heart will leap to my throat when the giant broad heads of bull sharks rise to the surface and snatch my snapper, boatside. Thick schools of long-beaked ballyhoo, spasmodic silver punctuation marks, will mob our chum-slick. I'll hear invisible flocks of shearwater bleating noisily as they migrate southward to the Caribbean. During rare west winds, I'll smell skunk foraging along the beach dunes for a meal. Beyond the reach of the worst light pollution on land, I'll track the constellations—Cassiopeia, Pleiades, Ursa Minor, Taurus—as they vault clear across the sky. Photoplankton will drift along the northward current at the surface, carpeting the calm sea in blue phosphorescence.

The human realm will never wholly disappear in our Atlantic. The lighthouse at the Hillsboro Inlet will wink at us from the south. Occasional vessels will motor past, festooned with deck and spreader lights. Low fireworks will sparkle landward more often than I'd ever expect. Airplanes, which we'll sometimes mistake for the lights atop sailboat masts, will blinker overhead. As Bill McKibben suggested quite a while back now in *The End of Nature* (1989), there's hardly a place left on earth where our human presence can't be felt. In south Florida, especially, we've forever altered the land, pasted it over with concrete and asphalt frosting. Yet tweaking my experience in the spatial and temporal realms—fishing the ocean in the dark—restores something essential to my state that hasn't been wholly lost, and draws me nearer too, somehow, to a more essential way of being in the world. I'll mostly finger the pulse of the nonhuman order taking over on shift-work when I meet darkest night close to its own terms on the Atlantic. It's amazing, all that I'd missed sealed behind doors at night inside my well-lit home.

"Hold the line while I get the truck," Tim commands this first night as we reach the ramp. It feels uncommonly good to stand once again on dry land. The dock feels unusually solid beneath my feet. My stomach seems to lower itself into its more comfortable grotto in my abdomen. *Just don't drop the line,* I warn myself for the second time tonight. As Tim runs off to retrieve the trailer, I look up at the heavy-lidded windows of the upscale condos. Everyone's long asleep. Except for me. Except for my fishing partner. Except for this strange sea at night.

5

Accidentals Happen

ACCIDENTAL. "A TERM USED TO DESCRIBE bird species which occur in a given place only very infrequently and irregularly," writes Christopher Leahy in *The Birdwatcher's Companion* (1982). South Florida, thanks largely to its proximity to the birdy tropics, hosts more than its share of accidentals, many of which seek shelter here on stopovers after braving tempestuous weather. One great thing about the World Wide Web, anyway, is its instant and global dissemination of such happenings. Birders routinely post accidental sightings on the Internet, and I've logged many an hour seeking to lay eyes, with varying success, upon these unexpected visitors: white-tailed kite (check), south polar skua (check), Cuban pewee (miss), Key West quail dove (check), bananaquit (miss), white-cheeked pintail (check; although some birders suspect that the specimen was a domesticated escapee), black-bellied whistling duck (check), Bahama mockingbird (check).

The most recent accidental I spotted in Florida was a least grebe (*Tachy-baptus dominicus*). Two of them were reported on the web by a couple of self-described "recreational" birders. They spotted the least grebes just a couple miles north of my home, in a small pond at the protected Yamato Scrub Natural Area, which at 217 acres is the largest remaining scrub tract in southern Palm Beach County. These high and dry scrublands—consisting mostly of sand pines, saw palmettos, dwarf oaks, and lichens—were among the first sites to be developed in south Florida, and only precious few acres remain. Yamato Scrub hosts several rare and endangered plants, including large-flowered rosemary, twisted and banded air plant, long strap fern, and Curtis' milkweed. The area also serves as critical habitat for several rare and endangered animals, including wood storks, gopher tortoises, eastern indigo snakes, and the Florida mouse. Threatened Florida scrub-jays used to breed on-site but haven't been seen in my area in years.

The smallest grebe in the Americas, least grebes also have the smallest range in the United States of any grebe (sometimes common names *do* make sense). A toe-tip curving into southern Texas from Mexico represents the extent of its North American grounds. The Cornell Lab of Ornithology claims that the least grebe is the least understood of the North American grebes, probably owing to both their limited range and their skulky grebe ways. Apparently, these particular grebes evade predators—and field biologists, I imagine—by hiding underwater with only their bills poking up for air. The least grebe may have developed this strategy to hide its most arresting physical feature, its eyes, which I've seen described as orange-yellow, yellow, or golden. In drawings, least grebe eyes stand out prominently against its black plumage and bill. I'm not sure what I find more dazzling: the brilliance of these eyes, so bright as to seem battery-powered, or their athletic efforts to conceal them. For habitat, the least grebe prefers weedy ponds or slow-moving streams, dense with vegetation. They dive for aquatic insect prey, primarily, but also eat algae. Come breeding season, nesting pairs will fight tenaciously with other least-grebe pairs for territory. The female lays three to six bluish-white eggs in a floating nest of aquatic vegetation, fixed in place by reeds. When they're not nesting, they can be found in small flocks.

The least grebes in Florida weren't very hard to spot. I brought the kids, Henry and Sophia, ten and eight years old at the time. A quick trot down the pine and oak-lined trail to an open area and the small pond, and there they were, impossible to miss or mis-identify. Small black birds going about their diving-grebe business at separate areas of the pond, their bright eyes—which seemed florescent yellow to me—were clearly visible through the binoculars. Like the pied-billed grebe, our more common and larger south Florida grebe, these least grebes darted beneath the water's surface with great speed, then bobbed up dramatically after their long dives, as if their tiny bodies were filled with helium. The genus name for grebes, appropriately, is a combination of two Greek words, those for "fast" and "sinking under." A group of grebes is known as a "water dance" of grebes. The inventive names we assign to groups of animals always fascinate, and sometimes confound, me. ("Murder" of crows?) Yet, given the sprightliness of the grebes I've observed, these least grebes included, "water dance" seems a perfectly apt description of these creatures. Someone who watched grebes and knew them well must have come up with this lovely group name.

"You see them, right?" I asked my kids, for fear that the birds would flit off at any moment back to south Texas. Henry and Sophia both nodded, said "uh-huh," and gazed at the small grebes through their binoculars once again. I could tell that they weren't sufficiently thrilled with our sighting.

"Do you realize how incredible this is, guys?" I pleaded with them. "Least grebes have only been sighted six times in the state of Florida in the past 100 years!"

"Wow," my son said, throwing me a bone.

Although I didn't appreciate it at the time, my kids may have been on to something with their muted reception. These weren't typical accidentals. The least grebes, that is, didn't flit off for home after a week, or a few days, or a month. Rather, they settled in and set up housekeeping. I returned to the pond several times over the next few months to keep tabs on the goings on. They built a small nest in the dense bulrushes at the pond's shore. Two eggs, other observers told me. The chicks hatched, and the black puff-balls were soon riding piggyback on both parents. Then, the chicks were swimming and diving on their own. These grebes, as I like to think my kids intuited, were living miraculously ordinary grebe lives by their lights—deliberate, purposeful lives. Just like us. My wife and I, after all, might also be seen as Florida accidentals. Like us, the least grebes were brought to this place by a set of circumstances, and they've tried to make the most of it. Nothing, my kids knew, to get excited over.

6

Snooking

DISCOVERING A FEW YEARS AGO that a fish called snook actually lurked beneath my feet in the sulfurous mangrove estuaries, concrete canals, and dredged inlets blocks from my home was sort of like when I discovered that a bird named snipe existed. I had to lay eyes on that skulking bird some ten years ago in a nearby wetland (and did, and do); I had to catch this fish (but haven't). It's not from a lack of trying.

I've done the research is the thing.

Centropomis undecimalis. Common name: snook. Salts pronounce its common name to rhyme with "Luke," but from the mouths of most anglers the name rhymes with "book." Snook range in color from amber to silver, depending on how much shrimp they've been eating. The snook boasts big yellowish fins. A dark lateral line streaks down the length of its body on both sides and accounts for one of its more popular aliases (linesider), while its long tapered head and underslung jaw accounts for another nickname (bucketmouth). It's common at eighteen to thirty-five inches long, but individuals may reach fifty-five inches and weigh nearly fifty pounds. Imagine a really long bass stretched absurdly at the snout before a funhouse mirror and you have the general idea.

"Livies," they say, work best. Try a pilchard, pinfish, mullet, or greenie, quivering beneath a popping cork. Or a brown shrimp pierced across its horny ridge on an eighth-ounce jig. Quarter-ounce in stiff current. Cut-bait works in a pinch. Ladyfish. Heads or tails. Or go artificial. Topwater plugs and poppers on cool mornings. Skitterwalk, zara spook, super spook, popa dog, glad-shad, bangolure, high rollers. Mind your retrieve. Walk the dog. Switch to suspending twitchbaits once the sweat beads on your lip. Bomber long A, goldeneye, cisco kid, X-rap, rat-l-trap, crystal minnow. Young guns favor soft plastics. Jerkbaits, Texas-rigged and weedless, dunked in Carolina lunker sauce. Paddletails, splittails, curlytails, shadtails, baitbusters, worms, frogs, what have you. Don't forget your colors. Natural presentations a good rule of thumb. Match the hatch. Rootbeer or motor oil for daylight dark bottoms; gold flake at night. Chartreuse, all else fails. Salts swear by white bodies and red heads. Salts use simple spoons too.

By this time, if anyone deserves to catch a linesider, I figure it's me. Yet I haven't gotten so much as a strike, a bite, a nibble, or even a window-shopper far as I can tell. Snook are still just a rumor to me, as much fuss as everyone seems to make over them. For I haven't so much as witnessed someone *else* catch one of these prized creatures. Instead, I've had my ear bent plenty, haunting my local boat docks and fishing piers.

"Best spot's at the spillway out west just north of Hillsboro," my first snook mentor declared at the Silver Palm Park boat ramp just ten minutes from my home. This was last winter. It was late at night and dark, when snook were purportedly hungry, less wary of hook, line, and leader, the terminal tackle less visible in any case under the sheet of darkness. The small park was abandoned, save for the mewling feral cats, the raccoons unabashedly mobbing the ripe rubber trash bins, and this black fisherman, who seemed to be about my age. I had noticed him a couple other times at the ramp, but hadn't yet mustered up the courage to interrupt his solitude. He sat that night, as usual, on an upside-down five-gallon bucket next to a hard plastic tackle-box, the size of a small coffin, his hefty rod poised in his soft grip over the intracoastal waterway, his gaze directed out toward the halo of boat-bothered water beneath his miner's headlamp. It was a cold night (by which I mean Florida brisk, 50s) so it caught my attention that he wore only his standard white, V-neck undershirt and navy work pants, and that he didn't seem cold. I planted myself a few respectful paces down from him, closer than I had previously dared, and struck up a mild conversation as I rigged my skinny rod, interspersing a battery of snook-related queries between remarks about the frosty weather, the passing boats, the opulent homes across the broad canal, the war in Iraq.

"So what's your name?" I asked, finally.

"Clarence," he said, and then he asked me my name, and then he divulged his favorite snook spot without my even asking, unusual for a fisherman. Maybe our perfectly ordinary exchange of first names had inspired the disclosure; or maybe he had simply given me the once-over, determined that the new white guy wearing baggy blue jeans and an impossibly clean sweatshirt emblazoned with the local university logo wouldn't likely provide much competition, fishing-wise.

"So if the best spot's out there at Hillsboro, why are you here? Is the light better?"

"Huh?"

Apparently, he didn't know the old joke to which I was alluding, which isn't really funny enough to explain here.

"Nothing," I said.

Before giving up and going home, I fished from the dock with Clarence for two or three hours, neither of us catching a darn thing—not so much as a crumby jack, spot, or grunt. It's something I've noticed about dock fishing in south Florida: it's tough going. You have to put in your time to catch much of anything for the dinner table, much less the single, slot-size keeper snook to which you're entitled during its short open seasons. The few swordfishermen rambling into the park that night in their souped-up trucks seemed to know this too and cast pitying looks our way as they lowered into the drink their behemoth offshore vessels, festooned with gargantuan electric reels and menacing gaffs.

The regulations for harvesting snook are far more restrictive, on the whole, than the regulations for swordfish. That said, you don't need a fancy boat or a big expensive rod to catch a snook. You don't even need a saltwater license if you fish from shore. Unlike the deep bluewater specimens mostly targeted by the Florida boat crowd—swordfish, mahimahi, tuna, wahoo—the snook haunt our inshore waters within easy range of beach, bridge, and dock, making themselves available to anyone with a rod and reel. While they treasure the mosquito-ridden redoubts deep in the 'glades, they also stack up to ambush prey in our most urban canals, making them one of the few inshore sport fish to have survived the rampant development along my urbanized stretch of inshore waterway, the cordgrass and spartina dredged up years ago to make room for deep-water boat channels, wooden docks, and concrete seawall. The snook's accessibility summons the broadest spectrum of Floridians, from genteel fly-fishermen who stalk their prey from costly technical poling skiffs to adolescent boys and girls who wet their lines in backyard canals along scruffy, weed-choked banks. It's the most democratic of fish. Which isn't to say that linesiders are easy to catch. Prone to what anglers call "lockjaw," snook are notorious for turning up their noses at a squirming shrimp plopped down perfectly in their field of view. I suppose you can say that the snook give everyone equal opportunity *not* to catch them.

Now that we play fair, anyway. Now that we use hook and line.

Truth is, the snook's inshore habitat—its cavorting with us primates—hasn't exactly played out to its advantage. During the 1940s and 1950s in Florida (the lean war years and those immediately following, when protein sources were scarce and of value), commercial harvesters deployed their haul-seines and gill-nets from shorelines with cataclysmic success. The Florida Fish and Wildlife Conservation Commission estimates that between 1941 and 1955, commercial fishermen harvested an average of nearly 500,000 pounds of snook, annually! The fish stock declined so rapidly during this period—mostly on account of the commercial harvest, partly on account of the rampant development just underway in Florida, transforming the snook's prized mangrove shoreline into concrete canal—that the state legislature instituted the first meaningful regulations in 1957, setting a recreational bag limit of four snook per day, making legal capture of snook by hook and line only, and closing the commercial snook fishery, entirely. If you've never heard of a fish called snook—as I hadn't until a few years ago—it's probably because you're not so long in the tooth and so the snook, unlike the swordfish, has never been a candidate for your dinner plate. Which doesn't mean it's not mighty tasty.

Snook boast ample "shoulders," which yield thick white fillets, succulent beyond compare—at least so I've heard. In *Sport Fish of Florida,* Dunaway describes the fillets as "mild yet flavorful . . . ranked at the top of nearly everyone's list of favorite fish." A quick Internet search reveals euphoric exchanges of snook recipes among anglers, including Vickie's snook parmesan, Lance Boutcher's snook sandwiches, barbecue snook, snook salad, herb-baked Florentine snook, beer batter snook, cajun snook, southwest Florida broiled snook, snook fillets with oyster sauce glaze. The Florida Fish and Wildlife Conservation Commission weighs in with its own culinary recommendations on its website, which appear, somewhat ironically, just after a paragraph on proper release procedures.

I catch and eat fish. It's part of what got me into this snook mess in the first place. Having lived in Florida for a decade, chastened by stories of commercial long-lines and depleted fish stocks (swordfish anyone?), and having read my Frances Lappé, my Michael Pollan, I decided that it was time to develop a more intimate relationship with my food. Some words of my wife's deceased stepmother, a vegetarian, also belatedly echoed in my mind. "My grandparents lived on a farm and slaughtered their own chickens," she had mentioned to me years ago over an impossibly spicy Indian meal she had prepared. "They tried to teach me to cut their throats, but I couldn't do it. I just figured if I couldn't kill them, I shouldn't eat them." The words didn't leave much of an impression on me at the time, but they began to clatter around inside my older skull. And so at about the same time I heard about the snook, I began to fish for yellowtail snapper with my colleague, Tim, who owned a small boat, whereupon I discovered something about myself. I *could* kill certain proteins, fish specifically. What's more, I could scale them, slit them throat to vent, scoop out their viscera with my fingers, free their fillets from their ribcages, spines, and skin with a slender, sharp blade, and bury their carcasses beneath my vegetable garden.

What did this mean? Up until a few years ago, birding had been my principal outdoors hobby, a decidedly low-impact, unbloody activity. Suddenly, I had become a fisherman too, which struck at least a few friends as a baffling development. "Fishing and birding"—a colleague in my department tasted the words in his mouth, a Cheshire grin surfacing on his face. "They sound the same, but they're not the same." A graduate student whom I introduced to Sartre, Peter Singer, and J. M. Coetzee wondered whether I had properly taken the "animal gaze" into account.

I get it, of course. I don't kill and eat the birds. I wield binoculars to admire the avian creatures, to exchange an uncomplicated gaze, not a gun to shoot them. Still, both birding and fishing root me to this place I now call home. Both activities put me in close contact, intimate contact, with separate outposts of my immediate environment, and a broader swath of the nonhuman and human persons inhabiting this place. It's this hunger for such contact, to know my place more fully, that accounts, I think, for the snook's current hold on my imagination.

After freeloading off my vessel-owning friend Tim for a couple years, I broke down and bought a boat. Not a deep-hulled offshore vessel like Tim's, but a small bay boat. The boat would allow me to head out of the inlet into the nearshore sea for snapper on calm nights, while its shallow draft and electric trolling motor would also permit me to stalk snook in skinny water branches here and there beyond the boat ramps and bridges. Clarence was my first fishing mate. I remembered that he had been the one to disclose his favorite snook spot. One good turn deserved another.

Clarence arrived at the dock our first night with the boat almost a half-hour late, his tired white Oldsmobile swinging around the one-way bend, lurching against its struts, fishing rods jutting out a back window. "That's my wife, Crystal," he said, pointing back to the car, not so much introducing his wife, who smiled toward me from the passenger's seat, as explaining her presence. "One of my girls there in back." I lifted a limp hand. "Hi there." Clarence wore what appeared to be the same uniform he always wore at the dock, the V-neck undershirt and work pants. As we loaded Clarence's coffin-size tackle box and heavy rods onto the boat, I couldn't help but notice that the Oldsmobile showed no sign of departing. The girl couldn't have been older than eight, and it was a school night.

"Are they just going to stay here, Clarence?"

"Yeah, they'll wait."

"I'd take them along, but—"

"Crystal don't like boats." He swatted his hand down as he spoke as if shooing away a pesky airborne insect. "She gets sea sick. They'll just fish from the dock."

We launched the boat and headed toward the inlet, drifting past the garish waterfront homes along the minimum-wake stretch of intracoastal. Clarence stood beside me at the console, gripping the stainless steel rail for ballast. It occurred to me, him standing close, that he was much shorter than he looked sitting on his bucket at the boat ramp the few times I had run into him there. We hadn't gotten halfway to the inlet before I learned that he resurfaced swimming pools for a living, that the work was sporadic and slow now, given the economic downturn, that he had nine (!) children—"all I wanted to do was lay 'em," he lamented of his youthful indiscretions with the mothers of his kids— that it was difficult to do right by all of them, but that he was trying, that the reason I hadn't seen him at the dock for a few weeks was because he had to go to jail for coldcocking a drunk at a Broward fishing dock who had laid his hands on Crystal's rear end, and that he "didn't mix much with his color."

It was a lot to absorb.

"Well, should we try for snook?" I inquired, steering our conversation into our more familiar waters. "Under the lights at the bridge piling? Or at the jetty, maybe?"

"Nah," Clarence scrunched up his face, shook his head. "They ain't around now. Too cold. They're holed up in shallow, stained water. Muddy bottoms. Won't eat worth a damn even if we find 'em. Let's just hit the reef."

Snook, like most creatures, are creatures of habit. And so Clarence, like most seasoned anglers, knew where and when we might find snook, what and whether they'd be eating. Yet it's taken scientists a long time to figure out the rhyme or reason of the snook's habits, and they still don't fully understand them all. Only after nearly decimating the snook population in this northern fringe of their tropical range did we decide—in the backward fashion that has long characterized our relationship with the nonhuman natural realm—that it would be a good idea to study its mysterious life cycle, in earnest. And so this much we know is true. Snook are protrandic hermaphodites, meaning they reverse their sex from male to female as they age and grow. Four distinct species of snook roam Florida's inshore waters: the fat snook, swordspine snook, tarpon snook, and the more common, common snook. Snook can live to be over twenty years old. Pretty long compared to the venerable mahimahi's paltry four-to-five-year life span. Snook stress easily, unlike their inshore cousins, the redfish, and so aquaculture efforts at Mote Marine Laboratory in Sarasota have been met with mixed results. Linesiders abide various salinity levels but don't tolerate the cold. A roughly horizontal "snook line" from Port Richey on the gulf coast to Cape Canaveral on the east coast marks the traditional northern boundary of snook habitat, as 54° F is considered the lowest water temperature they can tolerate. Even a rapid drop into the 60s . . . gone. Florida cold snaps in 1977, 1989, 2000, and 2010 have killed off thousands of snook. During winter, they favor the warmer shallow water and dark bottoms of inshore mangrove swamps and channels. As the days lengthen and the waters warm in spring, mature snook head oceanward to deepwater passes and inlets and remain there to spawn until September or so. Spawning picks up three days or so before the full moon and continues in earnest for only three days after the full moon. The small males bathe the larger females' eggs (over a million of them per "episode") in their frothy milt. Strong incoming tides channel the larvae inshore, where a lucky few fingerlings survive, hidden within the grassy bottoms and beneath the overhanging mangroves of the swamp. Juveniles migrate to salt marsh habitat and remain there for sixty to ninety days, then swim to seagrass beds, where they remain for up to five months, after which they decamp to various freshwater, brackish, and marine areas. Other than their temperature and spawning-induced travels, snook don't appear to be highly migratory. Still, linesiders tagged around Jupiter and Lake Worth in Palm Beach County have been recaptured in the Middle Keys. Jupiter-tagged snook have also been recaptured in Lake Okeechobee and in Charlotte Harbor clear across the peninsula, indicating that they had crossed the state from the Atlantic to the Gulf coast. What's more, big snook startle divers every so often at deep ocean reefs, slumming it with their snapper and grouper cousins.

That first night on the boat with Clarence, we anchored off the second reef from shore in about seventy-five feet of water. Once I felt the anchor line hold, I slipped a frozen block of menhaden chum inside its net, attached its line to a cleat, and lowered it into the thick ocean. Clarence set about his business while I flexed my back, took in the winter constellations, and took in Clarence. He dropped, rather than cast, his line—an enormous lead pyramid sinker below three separate hooks. Chicken-rig, I knew it was called. Tim had taught me a more subtle method of snapper-fishing, twelve-pound line and a small split-shot lead weight, which diverged dramatically from Clarence's method. Snapper were smart and wary. Not snook-smart, mind you, but pretty high up there on the fish-smart spectrum.

No sooner had Clarence's line hit bottom than he stood from his seat and began reeling in fast, his stout rod bent. Like the rig itself, there wasn't much subtlety in his retrieve, no play of the drag, which he must have set drumtight. He horsed in whatever bucked below, whirling in the line as he bowed at the waist over the gunwale, lowering the rod tip, then leaning back and lifting up a measure of line, putting all his weight into the exercise, his potbelly jutting from beneath the border of his tee shirt. Whirling and leaning . . . whirling and leaning . . . whirling and leaning. It was such a production that it surprised me when he plopped down two smallish white grunts onto the deck, one of which lived up to its name by snorting and snuffing as Clarence removed the hook from its narrow mouth with pliers. They were pretty creatures, really—turquoise tributaries winding from their snouts back toward their finlets, gleaming beneath Clarence's headlamp—but grunts all the same.

"You gonna throw those back?" I asked, lowering my own line.

"No, I'll keep 'em. Where's the cooler?"

I nodded toward the cooler seat with my head as my hands were occupied, feeding out my lighter line, which needed more active encouragement than Clarence's heavy rig. "You're gonna keep them?"

"An old lady in my neighborhood likes 'em. I'll take 'em for her."

"Oh," I said. "Sure. Okay."

As the night wore on, Clarence continued to pull up grunt after grunt, filling the cooler, as I fished with more limited success for snapper. There aren't any size or catch limits for grunts, as these plentiful reef fish—along with their cousins (margate, porgy, chub, squirrelfish, toro, etc.)—receive little fishing pressure. By contrast, the more prized snapper command a ten-fish aggregate bag limit per person.

"You're gonna have to go lighter if you want to catch any yellowtail," I finally urged Clarence. "I think your neighbor has enough grunts." It was getting late and I had caught only two keeper snappers. Small ones at that. I wanted Clarence to catch at least one quality fish for himself. Plus, I wouldn't have minded him catching enough snappers to supplement my own meager efforts.

"I'm all right," he uttered.

It was time to pack it in once midnight arrived. I had caught my two keeper snappers to what must have been Clarence's twenty-five grunts. *Twenty-five grunts. Two measly snappers.* I had entertained higher hopes for my fishing partner's expertise. But maybe he didn't know so much about fishing the reef.

I gave Clarence my cell-phone number that first night out on the boat, and he took to calling me about once a week. "We goin' out tonight?" he'd ask. I couldn't always, or even mostly, say yes. My day job, filial responsibilities (e.g., soccer practice, swimming practice, boy scouts), and outsize sleeping requirements limited the number of late-nights I could handle. Plus I had a couple other fishing partners calling dibs. But I took Clarence out a few more times last winter and we pretty much repeated the same choreography. He usually arrived late, his beat-up sedan lurching around the one-way park entrance, as I fiddled with my cleat lines, rearranged ice bags in the coolers, and stewed. Sometimes his wife, and one or two of his young children, waited or napped in the car, or fished from the dock, and sometimes he came alone. We slow-trolled for snook beneath the intracoastal bridges a few times, threw some bait beside bridge pilings, but mostly we headed out to the reef, where we stood a greater chance of actually catching fish. He horsed in dozens of grunts—for his elderly neighbor—and I caught fewer snapper, sometimes giving him one or two.

And then Clarence disappeared. I tried calling him on his cell phone after not hearing from him for a month or so, as February gave way to March. "Snook'll be coming back any time now," I tempted him with a message. "It's warming up. Call me, buddy." But he didn't call, and I stopped seeing him at the boat ramp at night. Every once in a while that spring I'd see a black fellow sitting on a plastic bucket, who looked something like Clarence. I'd approach, only to recognize as I neared that it wasn't Clarence, but someone else, horning in on one of my friend's favorite spots. I tried calling Clarence a couple more times and was finally greeted by one of those annoying automated voices over the phone line telling me that the number had been disconnected.

I don't want to misrepresent things. Part of me was relieved when Clarence vanished. Our fishing partnership—given the combination of his hectoring to go out and his tardiness when I could—was inconvenient, for one thing. Plus, a mild discomfort attended each of our outings as we shared so little in common. Yet something, something beyond any lingering sense of obligation, kept me searching for Clarence, kept me interested in him. Perhaps *because* we shared so little in common, *because* a mild discomfort attended each of our outings. To fish with Clarence was to immerse myself, if only for a time, in a strange and new local vocabulary, and I must have recognized something of value in this immersion. Florida, and its fish, and fishing, meant something different to Clarence than it meant to me. It meant more to him, I think I knew, cut closer to the bone, even though I hadn't yet thought about it enough—nor, maybe, had I talked to Clarence enough when I had the chance—to truly see Clarence, to understand as fully as I might the contours of his unique relationship with his homeplace. He fished for food. Which is different than simply eating one's catch, as I do.

The snook, standing in for Clarence last spring, predictably returned from their inshore winter digs to the intracoastal, the inlet, and the beaches. I finally saw what I'm pretty certain was a school of them, big females, stacked up like copper logs beside the lit-up bridge piling at the inlet. Incoming tide. Clear water. They undulated there, six feet down or so, doing a better job of holding their place in the stiff current to ambush their prey than I was managing to do in my small boat to ambush mine. I cast an artificial shrimp lure in their general direction between my harried negotiations of the steering wheel and throttle but managed to set the bait down into the zone only a couple times. They weren't having any of it. After nearly colliding with one vessel charging through the narrow corridor beneath the bridge, I gave up and headed out the inlet for snapper. "Frickin' snook," I uttered to my fishing partner, Tim, out with me that night; he didn't care much about catching snook. Clarence might have known how to catch them, I thought. He had told me that the big females at this heavily fished spot had seen it all and were especially smart and wary. "That's how they get to be big females in the first place," he had said. The snook were here now, at least. But where the hell was Clarence?

There were any number of places that he might have been, and might still be. He might be haunting other boat ramps, docks, and piers in Broward; he might have moved closer to Miami or the Keys, places he'd mentioned to me where he enjoyed the fishing even more. He might be in jail. He might be dead, for all I know.

It's been over a year now since I've heard from Clarence. The snook, meanwhile, continue to maintain their powerful hold over my imagination. I think about them all the time—embarrassingly often, really—whenever I light out to the boat ramp, whenever I pass beneath the inlet bridge, and often during those blessed few unhurried moments of my day when my mind simply wanders. I've got snook on the brain. For reasons not altogether clear to me, however, I've pretty much given up on the linesider as a fishing target. Every once in a while I'll throw a plug or plastic shrimp toward a seawall or a lit dock, but only in an obligatory way. I ponied up the extra $2 this year to renew the special snook permit on my saltwater fishing license, but I know I wouldn't harvest (i.e., kill) a snook even if by some miracle I caught one during open season and within its narrow legal slot-size. It may be that I don't want to catch a snook. More, that I've never truly wanted to dupe a linesider into striking my barbed offering, on account of what the snook simply *is*. Smart. Strange. Scarce. Dear. Too smart, strange, scarce, and dear for the lowly likes of a fisherman like me.

In the meantime, I've become something of a snapper specialist. It's been a tough winter for snapper, though. Tougher even than last winter with Clarence, when I'd catch only two or three keepers, and sometimes none, per outing. They've been scarce as snook. We've endured several cold snaps is the problem, water temps in the mid-60s. "The yellowtail are gone, I'm afraid," Tim lamented on one of our luckless nights last month between cold fronts. All we seemed to be catching were grunts. "We should really try one," he suggested, throwing a specimen over the gunwale, back into the Atlantic. "They're really not so bad, I hear. Sort of bony." I thought immediately of Clarence, and those manifold grunts—white, french, and bluestriped—he caught on my boat those few times, maybe for his elderly neighbor, as he claimed, but likely, it only then occurred to me, thick as I am, for the many younger mouths he had to feed, the ones he was trying, anyway, to do right by.

7

Neighboring Gardens

I HAD A FIGHT WITH MY NEIGHBOR a while back. Not an actual fight. It didn't come to fisticuffs. Rather, it was the type of fight you'd expect from someone who'd summon up the word "fisticuffs." It was a fairly typical verbal dispute between suburban neighbors, carried out over the shared wooden fence between our modest properties, a fence we had recently replaced after Hurricanes Frances and Jeanne decimated the original six-foot boundary, leaving us feeling naked and exposed.

"Andy?" I heard my neighbor's voice address me from over the solid new partition. He must have heard me rustling around in my scraggly butterfly and bird garden.

"Yeah, Franco?" I answered, standoffish, my timbre unpleasantly harsh even to my own ears. I think I'm a pretty friendly person—I try to be, anyway—but it's been hard to be friendly with my neighbors, Franco and Paola. They're Italian immigrants who own a nursery west of the city bordering the Everglades. They've lived in the neighborhood longer than we have, they keep their property "up" the way you'd expect nursery owners to keep their property up, and from the moment we moved in next door they've pressured my wife and me to adhere to their fastidious example. Brusquely. On the rare occasions when Franco addresses me, I know that it's only to exhort me to edge my tough grass more neatly off the sidewalk, to unearth a shrub whose roots, he claims, threaten to buckle his sprinkler lines, or to prune my firebush or lime tree, whose arms I've allowed to stretch brazenly over the invisible plane above our shared fence. Their twin sons often hoist fallen palm fronds, which stray occasionally from our royal and sabal palms, back over the tall fence onto our property (I've seen them), plopping the broad fronds right on top of our milkweed plants, sometimes. What's more, I do much of my work at home and they're awfully loud neighbors. Both husband and wife tend to holler at each other quite a bit, and at their sons, broadcasting vague domestic rancor in their native tongue to the entire neighborhood. The extravagant Italian glottals seemed almost charming when we first moved in, but the charm rapidly dissipated.

All of which I hope partly explains, if not excuses, my surly, *Yeah, Franco?*

"You take down bird feeder," he declared more than asked. In fairness, Franco's English isn't exactly terrific. It's nebulous terrain, his intended tone. Still . . .

"No. I'm not taking it down. Why would I do that?"

"Squirrels all over my garden because feeder. They eating all our tomatoes."

If Franco could have seen my expression over the fence, I wouldn't have had to use words to respond. But we were invisible to each other.

"Franco. Come on. Be serious. The squirrels live in the oaks all over the neighborhood." Here, I pointed (stupidly, as Franco couldn't see me) to the majestic specimen looming over my property from a separate neighbor's yard. "They didn't find your tomatoes because of my bird feeder." I was pretty certain about this, even though an obnoxious tribe of squirrels did loiter around my scruffy butterfly and bird garden. As Franco had figured out, they lustily consumed my feeder's black oil sunflower seeds, despite my best efforts to thwart their access.

"It would be nice for us to have one tomato this year, at least."

Franco's final statement pierced me, yet I held my ground, partly because I couldn't imagine that the squirrels would simply stop eating his tomatoes if I removed my sunflower seeds. If the varmints had a yen for tomatoes, tomatoes they'd eat. The controversy also seemed to crystallize our conflicting notions of land management, generally, which only steeled my resolve. My son, Henry, would come along and complicate these feelings. But here I'm getting ahead of the story. For at the time, my biocentric notions, albeit vague, held sway.

Upon moving to Florida and buying our first home, my wife and I endeavored to put our environmental notions into practice on our small patch of sandy Florida soil. There was a lot to do. Foremost, we would dig up as much of that useless St. Augustine grass as possible. The chemical fertilizers, insecticides, and weed-killers necessary to maintain the green carpet, the precious water depleted through the sprinkler lines, the poisonous carbon emissions spewed from a two-stroke mower, the coarseness of these particular leaves of grass beneath our bare feet, a pugnacious variety that would have left Walt Whitman wanting for poetic inspiration . . . it was a wonder to us that *anyone* cultivated this stuff in south Florida. We'd supplant the St. Augustine, and the few existing beds of ornamental annuals—impatiens, begonias, portulaca, periwinkle—and replace them with native trees and perennial shrubs, with an eye toward supporting whatever local animals were still fighting the good fight along our increasingly urbanized coastal ridge, sandwiched between the Atlantic Ocean and the embattled Everglades.

For the cost of mere postage and handling, the Florida Game and Fresh Water Fish Commission sent us a useful manual, *Planting a Refuge for Wildlife: How to Create a Backyard Habitat for Florida's Birds and Beasts,* which guided us toward specific trees and shrubs. Armed with a theory, we've gradually replaced the non-native specimens and most of the grass with live oak, gumbo limbo, firebush, geiger tree, milkweed, necklace pod, privet, wild coffee, simpson stopper, cassia, lantana, plumbago, golden dewdrop, salvia, coontie, and marlberry. As I catalogue these plantings—surveying our small yard in my mind's eye—it occurs to me that our property sounds more glorious here than it actually looks. The cumulative result of all this work, in truth, is a front and back yard that probably seems unkempt to the untrained (or differently trained) eye, which brings me back to my nursery-owning neighbors.

When Hurricanes Frances and Jeanne struck, laying waste to our wooden fence, my wife and I got our first good look at the property next door. Their small yard pretty much conformed to our expectations. There weren't too many plants to speak of—for one thing it was too early in the season for winter gardening, plus we had just weathered two strong hurricanes—but the plantings that had endured were ornamental, low-lying specimens, shorn into neat geometric forms and larger patterns. Thorns shot from several of the rugged specimens. Aggressively dyed mulch and small pebbles of manifold color demarcated boundaries between particular garden beds. I wasn't certain about the identities of the plants, but I was pretty sure that they wouldn't be found in our *Planting a Refuge for Wildlife* manual. The north side of their property seemed to be reserved for their herb and vegetable pursuits. There was room only for a few raised beds, bordered in perfect rectangles by heavy wooden beams. An elaborate metal scaffolding for beans or peas had survived the storms no worse for the wear; rows of twine stretched vertically across the structure as if it were a giant musical harp. *Control*, on the whole, seemed to be the yard's principal motif. Their sole tree—shorn of most of its clothes by the fierce winds—was a star fruit tree, the perfect citrus ode, I thought, to their strict geometric preferences. Small wonder that our neighbors couldn't countenance our apparent courting of the squirrels, these utterly uncontainable, uncontrollable creatures.

At the time of my verbal confrontation with Franco, my wife and I felt that we stood on pretty solid moral ground. We enjoyed gardening, like our neighbors, but whereas their aesthetic and dietary pleasure seemed their only guiding principal, we prided ourselves on our less anthropocentric criteria. Over the years, we tried intermittently to raise tomatoes too, but only casually and unsuccessfully. We weeded haphazardly and sprayed the plants on occasion with an organic insecticidal soap, which did little to impede or even distract the countless variety of subtropical pests. We'd managed to harvest an edible tomato or two, but mostly our gardens nourished the outside animals, which had been fine by us. It's not as if we were actual farmers. Who were we to deprive the squirrels of the fruits of our garden? And who did Franco think he was, I thought, uncharitably, pressuring us now to remove our bird feeder? "Can you believe that guy?" I argued as Wendy shook her head slowly, punctuating my own exasperation.

Then Henry, as I've suggested, had to go and complicate matters. Out of the blue this past fall, our son decided that he would take a more active role in our sloppy vegetable garden. Gardening, we immediately thought, would be a solid enterprise for him. It would encourage those nurturing and contemplative impulses paid short shrift by the more dominant cultural influences swirling around our son in today's boy culture. "Persuade a careless, indolent man to take an interest in his garden, and his reformation has begun," Susan Fenimore Cooper, James Fenimore Cooper's daughter, declares in her underappreciated 1850 book, *Rural Hours*. Cooper wasn't thinking of video games and iPads when she referenced the scourge of thoughtless laziness, but her general view of gardening as a salutary, countercultural force for men still rings pretty true.

Henry's interest in gardening was a likely development, in any case. He's a shy child who enjoys concentrating upon tactile endeavors (e.g., the disembowelment and haphazard reassembly of any electronic device he can get his hands on) that don't require direct verbal communication with other people. We figured that he would enjoy gardening and that his communication with the soil might also provide him with certain talking points that he could fall back upon when cornered into a conversation by relatives or peers (*Sure, the Nintendo DS is pretty cool, but have you checked out the new packets of Clemson Spineless Okra seeds?*). Further, it must be said that Henry relishes food, so much so that he plans his school lunches weeks in advance. It would be a valuable lesson, surely, for him to learn firsthand what it takes to produce, well, produce.

Moreover, how fitting that he pursue this activity in our particular state, Florida. While outsiders might not think immediately of Florida when they think of agricultural U.S. states, you could make a pretty convincing case that the Sunshine State is our most crucial agricultural state. Thanks largely to our year-round growing season, Florida, according to our state's Department of Agriculture and Consumer Services website, ranks first in the United States in the value of production of sugarcane and most citrus varieties, as one would expect, but also ranks first in the value of production of snap beans, fresh-market tomatoes, cucumbers for fresh market, squash, bell peppers, watermelons, and sweet corn, as one might not expect. Most of the acreage right around our feet in Boca Raton, as I explained to Henry, was once farmland. African Americans from the historic Pearl City neighborhood just blocks away worked the pepper, bean, and tomato fields at Butts Farm and Strickland Farm, where our swanky local mall now stands, at Frank Chesebro's property, supplanted by the famous Boca Raton Resort and Club, and at the Raulerson Farm, replaced by the Army Air Field during World War II, which later yielded to our private airport and to the public university where I now work. While most, though not all, of Boca Raton's farmland has been muscled out by commercial and residential real-estate ventures, Henry's modest wintertime garden would retrieve this local legacy and express, in miniature, larger Florida's ongoing wintertime agricultural efforts.

Suddenly, we had a lot riding on this garden. Too much, I might have discerned. Things started off okay. Our vegetable garden, such as it was, was located along a narrow strip of our property on the east side of the house, the side opposite our border with the Italian nursery owners. Upon Henry's prodding, we ripped out a broader tract of that useless St. Augustine grass to offer him a twenty-foot-by-six-foot plot, a size that seemed to strike a clean bargain between our son's outsize ambition and what was practicable. I can't say I was overwhelmed by Henry's work ethic when it came to manual labor—my wife and I performed most of the heavy lifting—but he did his share by carrying piles of the stiff uprooted grass to the curb for foliage pick-up day. His little sister, Sophia, also pitched in by collecting the worms that we had unearthed and reserving them for later distribution. Neither of our children are squeamish about creepy-crawly things, such as the snakes, lizards, and bugs so prevalent in their subtropical home.

After we cleared and tilled the plot of sandy soil, we drove to our local nursery (okay, Home Depot) and began our shopping in earnest. My father-in-law, who leads a rather self-sufficient, light-footed existence on his large property in the Pennsylvania sticks, mailed us his extra copy of the behemoth classic, *The Encyclopedia of Organic Gardening,* first published by Pennsylvania's Rodale Press in 1959. So we knew enough to strive for "a fair amount of humus" in the soil while also maintaining a "light and porous" consistency. As our native sandy soil was plenty porous but nutritionally parched, we loaded plenty of peat moss, manure, and rich garden soil onto our flatbed carts to offer the ground a healthful boost. Regarding pests, our organic encyclopedia endorsed the hand-picking and kerosene-dousing of hornworms, etc., which seemed a rather macabre enterprise. Thankfully, the authors also touted "Some easy-to-make sprays, such as red pepper or onion and garlic." My father-in-law, I knew, powdered his plants with heady doses of cayenne pepper to keep the groundhogs, deer, and rabbits at bay. He also urinated frequently all about the perimeter of his large garden plots, fortified by his copious intake of Pennsylvania pilsners and porters. Striking a vague compromise, Wendy plucked a bottle of organic insecticidal soap concentrate (comprising mostly sesame and fish oils) from a shelf a few aisles over from the peat, manure, and soil.

Next, we were on to the actual plants. We bought some seeds but mostly seedlings to give Henry a head start. Naturally, our boy gravitated toward the vegetables and fruits he savored, piling a promiscuous assortment of tiny plastic pots onto our carts. Whereas Wendy and I had planted only tomatoes and herbs in past seasons, now we were apparently in for Ichiban and Black Beauty eggplants, Early Snowball A cauliflower, Evergreen Long White Bunching onions, and Clemson Spineless okra, as Henry savors Indian cuisine, plus a medley of peppers to complement our boy's appreciation for Mexican food: habaneros, jalapenos, hot bananas, anaheim, poblano, and cayenne. "Whoa, easy on the peppers," I advised as Henry reached for a second raft of tiny poblano plantings. "How many chili rellenos do you think we can eat?" Suddenly, our two flatbed shopping carts were fully loaded, and we hadn't even gotten to the tomatoes. By the time we checked out, we had managed to limit the quantity, if not the diversity, of Henry's pepper selections, as well as to incorporate into the mix Long Imperator #58 carrots, Catskill Brussels sprouts, Detroit Dark Red beets, Pink Beauty radishes, parsley, and several tomato varieties.

We returned home, prepared the soil, and nestled the seeds and seedlings into their beds. We didn't exactly adhere to best-practices when it came to the spacing in our overpopulated garden, but we at least tried to locate the specimens that would grow taller toward the north side of the plot so that they wouldn't shade their neighbors. Depleted and filthy, we left it to Henry to douse the new seeds and plantings with a light shower of water. "Now let's not get too excited," I tried to check Henry's expectations as he showered his plot. "We've never planted all these peppers and stuff, and you know how success-ful we've been with the tomatoes," I added, sarcastically. "I'm not sure how it'll come out. What happens happens."

Henry shrugged his shoulders and nodded, offering his grudging consent. But it was clear to me that a failed garden simply wouldn't do this year. And so, after mysterious subtropical pests aboveground and grotesque, translucent grubs below began devouring the foliage and root systems of our tomatoes and okra, I did something that I'm not particularly proud of. Reader, I used a chemical pesticide, Sevin to be precise. The Zone 6 sensibilities that inform *The Encyclopedia of Organic Gardening*, I'm afraid, didn't quite translate to our Zone 10 realities. Control, suddenly, climbed up the gardening criteria on our side of the fence, the X-factor of our son's feelings in the mix.

"Sevin's not so bad, really," my father-in-law uttered over the telephone line, consoling me. "There's a lot worse out there." He was certainly correct on this score. *The Complete Guide to Florida Gardening* (1987), a popular Florida gar-dening book given to us as a gift a few years ago, recommends treating tomato plots with Vapam, a soil fumigant accompanied by a voluminous and down-right terrifying menu of toxic hazards, including chronic pulmonary edema, coma, and death. Thankfully, the product was taken off the retail market a few years back, although it's still in use among commercial farmers.

I'd like to report that Henry was an industrious little gardener during the following weeks as October gave way to November, as November gave way to December, that he spent hours carefully tending his plants. But this wasn't exactly the case. Barbara Kingsolver, one of our more passionate family gar-deners, has noted that one of the principal virtues of a garden is that it offers children the rare opportunity in our contemporary society to feel, and be, useful. Yet our son never developed much of a passion for pruning or weeding, or for securing the rapidly growing tomato plant tendrils to their stakes and cages with additional gardening tape, or for plucking the unproductive "sucker" stems that sprouted at a randy rate. I had to prod him to perform these necessary, useful chores. Instead, Henry spent most of his time simply observing the goings on in his garden plot, from what I could gather observing him from time to time from the window of his sister's room. On his bare knees, he'd trace the migration of a strange bug as it made its way across the patch of soil, then gather the courage to pluck up the creature for closer inspection. Sometimes, his eyes seemed to train on a particular plant for an awfully long time, as if he were observing its growth in real time.

And grow the plants did, just as they were supposed to do. I couldn't help being somewhat surprised by our initial success. I hadn't ever grown anything but tomatoes and herbs. It struck me as pretty miraculous when our ostensible okra seedlings raced ahead of their competitors in the garden to grow into actual okra plants advertising audacious yellow blooms with purple centers, then the tiny green tips of the okra pods, themselves, bursting through their sheaths.

"How about that," I uttered to my wife as we surveyed the goings on one day. "Okra." Wendy, raised in rural Pennsylvania, flashed me a look I can only describe as bemused condescension.

"What, exactly, were you expecting?" she inquired.

Over the next few weeks, the okra plants continued to produce okra, the eggplants produced eggplant, the peppers produced peppers, the tomatoes produced tomatoes. Brussels sprout beads bloomed at the elbows of the tough rangy Brussels sprout plants; cauliflower heads swelled within the secretive leaves of cauliflower plants. It was tough to know exactly what was going on with the onions and carrots beneath the soil, but we figured that things were proceeding apace. Everything was going pretty well until we hired our regular tree trimmer, Willie, to prune some fronds off our sabal palm to allow more sunlight through to the garden. My wife, our daughter, Sophia, and I had retreated to the house while Willie worked; but Henry, evidently, had remained behind to keep watch. Before we knew it, we heard the sliding glass door screech open upon Henry's urgent command.

"Look!" he uttered, brandishing a limp green plant in his meaty paw. A poblano plant, I was pretty sure. We could still hear the sound of Willie's chainsaw whirring in the background. Hot tears streamed down Henry's cheeks. The skin beneath and around his eyebrows was red and enraged, as it tends to get during his fiercest crying jags. He's awfully quick to tears, our son, a cause of some concern to us. He's also quick to hug. We've tried to moderate both of these impulses as Henry has grown older. His teachers have expressed concern that other boys will begin teasing him if they see him melt down over something small, or if they see him hugging the principal. He's in fourth grade, after all, and incredibly tall for his age, too. And he's a boy. But it's hard to know how fiercely we should regulate his hugs, or his tears. It took Wendy and me a long time to intuit that hugs and tears operate partly as surrogates for the words that simply won't come to Henry.

"Great! Just great!" our son continued, tears still streaming down his cheeks.

I rushed out the sliding glass door to address the calamity. "Willie!" I shouted, waving my arms. "Stop!" He glanced down at me from atop his ladder and lowered his chain saw, awaiting an explanation.

The garden was a catastrophe, our tender plants buried beneath the chaos of broad palm leaves and coarse nets of their seeds. Henry took one more look at the plot and retreated back inside, muttering wicked oaths, unable to bear the sight of the carnage. With Willie's help, I gingerly removed the debris, as if seeking to locate earthquake victims from beneath the rubble. Thankfully, the damage wasn't nearly as great as I feared. The poblanos had suffered the worst of it, several of them mortally wounded, but most of the eggplants and okra in this southernmost section of the garden had been spared, sheared stems here and there. After tidying things up a bit, I retrieved Henry, who still clenched the wilted remains of his poblano plant in his grip, to show him that things weren't actually so bad. We had lost only a few plants, I assured him. The others would grow back in no time. He nodded his head, sniffling back tears. The plants, I realized then, weren't just plants to Henry, whatever "just plants" means. They were something more.

Henry's relationship with his garden plants came into greater focus a few weeks later once we harvested our first head of cauliflower. We gave Henry the honors. Brandishing our dull garden knife, he sawed through the main stem at the base just inside the leaf shell and, after considerable effort, freed the big bumpy vegetable. That night, Henry helped me to prepare a pretty delicious aloo gobi, spiced with cumin, coriander, turmeric, and even one of our jalapeno peppers. The trouble came the next morning when it was time to unearth the hollow remains of the cauliflower plant.

"Well," I said, leaning over the depleted cradle of leaves with a trowel. "Time to dig up the cauliflower plant and put it in the compost heap."

"What!?" Henry asked, the scaffolding of his face giving way. Then, "No!"

It hadn't occurred to Henry that it was once-and-out for a cauliflower plant, this plant that he'd spent so much time with over the past several weeks. It was inconceivable to him that the poor plant, his companion, would be uprooted and dispatched so violently with the blade of my trowel. Were such drastic measures necessary?

Of course, I inferred all of this from Henry's panicked expression, from his "What!?" and his "No!" but I'm pretty sure I got the gist of what he meant.

Hoping to dispense some fatherly wisdom, I told him that it was only a plant, that it didn't feel pain, not having feelings at all, that it wasn't like it was a friend or something, all the while feeling rather crappy about the things that I was saying. How do we really know, after all, that plants don't feel pain? It certainly would have *preferred*, anyway, to remain in the soil. Who was I, moreover, to define "friend" for Henry?

A garden, I slowly began to learn during our first season with Henry's garden, could mean more to someone than I had ever fathomed. It could be a site for the production of food, or a site to inspire aesthetic delight, or a site to occupy one's hands in useful labor, or a site in which one might carry out biocentric principles. It could be all of these things, of course, but it could be other things too. To my son, his garden was a functional society, above all, a collection of individual citizens, all of whom mattered deeply to him. Maybe this was partly true of my Italian neighbors, also. Maybe they cared more about their defenseless tomato plants' feelings, under siege by the squirrels, than they let on, or even fully knew. Or, more likely, it *was* all about control with them.

But maybe this wasn't quite so inexcusable.

Paola's father, I learned from my neighbor Franco in the middle of our garden season, had passed away in Sicily right about the time of our verbal altercation over my bird feeder. A holiday block party and its attendant alcohol had inspired a rare moment of civil, even friendly, conversation between us. The father had been gravely ill for months, a continual source of guilt and stress upon Paola, which, I gathered over my beer, surely must have accounted for a fair amount of the hollering from across the fence at that time. Franco, himself, I learned next, had suffered a heart attack shortly thereafter and had undergone a bypass operation. Perhaps a neat and tidy garden had offered both Paola and Franco a measure of sanity far from home amid a dizzying alien culture, amid a host of immediate circumstances so utterly out of their control. Their plants might have been non-natives, but so were they; so was I. Perhaps I could be less hostile toward Florida's human, *and* plant, immigrants. Paola and Franco certainly weren't planting invasive species, as rigorously as they pruned them. Perhaps some familiar, tidy plants could be excused.

Perhaps one measly tomato wasn't too much for them to expect.

Subjecting a neighbors' garden and a son's garden to such scrutiny forces you to take a harder look at your own peccadilloes. So what about my own scraggly bird and butterfly garden, which couldn't look more different from my neighbors' garden, or Henry's garden on the other side of the house? For all of my lofty biocentric principles—my professed advocacy of Florida's undervalued native plants—perhaps more selfish, primitive impulses truly inform my landscaping choices. In most respects, after all, I lead a life all too contained, domesticated, and tame. So is my unruly native garden more truly my way of living life on the wild side some? I don't generally lament my domestication, and so it's probably a good thing that the resistance of my inmost giant expresses itself freely in my garden, alone. Yet these impulses undergirding my gardening preferences may be just as visceral and self-indulgent as the motivations of my neighbors.

I'd chalk up Henry's first season as principal gardener as an unqualified success, accented by small sublime moments: a call from Henry's grandmother asking him to supply the parsley for their Passover Seder; two enormous, gleaming eggplants bearing the curious profiles of Easter Island statues, which we only reluctantly sliced, fried, and savored; the good-natured argument between our two kids over who would get to eat our first carrot; the live oak sapling that volunteered smack in the middle of his plot; and the short paragraph that Henry wrote about his garden on his application to attend a gardening sleepover camp in upstate Florida this summer. Henry struggled through the modest writing assignment, laboring over his few words, gripping his pencil within his white knuckles. But he managed. "I like gardens and plants," he scrawled. "I want to learn about plants and how to grow them. I have a garden at my house. I want to know which plants help each other out."

The paragraph smacks of Henry's typical understatement. Despite his teacher's prodding, he rarely incorporates what she calls "juicy" verbs and adjectives into his prose. All the same, his vision of a garden as a functional society of individual citizens comes through in his last sentence. It would be difficult, indeed, for me to overstate my son's actual enthusiasm for his garden. My wife and I now have to be careful about the things we leave strewn around the house in plain view, because Henry now confiscates any concave objects he can lay his hands on—plastic drinking cups and yogurt containers, beach pails, spice jars, his sister's depleted watercolor trays, and so on—fills these receptacles with potting soil and seeds, and sets them out somewhere, anywhere, on our property where they might garner a few hours of precious sunlight and rain. He's discovered on his own, after raiding our recycling bin, that plastic water bottles make great homes for onion bulbs once he shears off their narrow plastic tops. While he still doesn't like weeding much, Henry's pretty industrious about setting out five-gallon buckets under the eaves to capture rare winter rainwater for his plants.

The depth of Henry's love for gardening emerged most forcefully at a recent Easter egg hunt, which a neighbor of ours organizes each year at our local park, and from which we've never had the heart to exclude our Jewish kids. After Henry opened his designated giant egg this year—which we filled with various seed packets and a disposable soil-testing kit—he turned to us and declared, without any trace of inherited sarcasm, "This is the best day of my life." Here was another moment when I felt duty-bound to intervene and dispense fatherly wisdom—to let Henry know that the seeds and soil-tester kit had cost us only a few dollars, that the gift wasn't really a big deal, that he needn't feel so grateful. However, I managed to keep my fat mouth shut, and I'm glad that I did. Henry will learn soon enough, I know, that the electronic gizmos tucked in his peers' Easter eggs cost more than his seed packets did. But I'd rather that he live a bit longer in a world where he can assign his own sense of worth to things.

As for our Italian neighbors, it was Henry who found a pretty solid solution to our bird feeder impasse. "We need to get a Twirl-a-Squirrel," he declared one morning after I urged him over breakfast to chase a squirrel off our feeder. He uttered the suggestion without much enthusiasm or even emphasis, and so I didn't take his comment seriously. But then he invoked the phrase again, Twirl-a-Squirrel, the next time I pleaded with him to shoo off a pesky squirrel. Turns out, the Twirl-a-Squirrel is an actual product. Henry had read about it in one of the many seed catalogues he now studies like scripture. We sent away for the small battery-operated device, and it works like a charm, twirling the feeder counterclockwise at a rate just fast enough to expel the clinging rodents. I'm not sure that Franco or Paola have noticed our new device, or that the fewer squirrels at our feeder has limited the number of squirrels mobbing their tomatoes, but it sure has increased the number of painted buntings that we've seen this season. While I hope I've done right by our neighbors, I've also tried to do right by the poor squirrels. After refilling the feeder each time, I've taken to sprinkling a cupful of seeds on the ground, a good distance away from our neighbor's property. A peace offering, of sorts, to the varmints, and one of my several tortured attempts to negotiate what I perceive as the conflicting demands of my suburban citizenship. I can't speak for the birds or for my rangy plants or for the more upright vegetable citizens on Henry's side of the house; I can't speak for my Italian neighbors or even for my son. But I like to think that the squirrels, at least, appreciate my efforts.

8

Burrowing Owls

"SUPPOSEDLY, THEY LIKE AIRPORTS," a student of mine declared, confused furrows sprouting like parentheses between her brows. Pity the poor misunderstood burrowing owl (*Athene cunicularia*). My student, new to bird-watching, was excited to see these long-legged owls on our university campus standing beside their burrows. She immediately consulted Roger Tory Peterson's *A Field Guide to the Birds* (1934): "Habitat: Open grassland, prairies, farmland, airfields."

I explained to her—at least 80 percent sure that I knew what I was talking about—that the struggling burrowing owls didn't actually *like* airports, or even farmland for that matter. Rather, so much of their native habitat having been pasted over by concrete and asphalt frosting, the relatively unconstructed terrain adjacent to airports and farmland probably came closest to approximating their preferred grassland and prairie. Here's the Boca Raton burrowing-owl narrative in a nutshell, which approximates their story throughout their U.S. range: the owls favored the dry prairie over the bean and pepper fields that encroached in the first decades of the twentieth century; they would have preferred the prairie, too, over the World War II Army air field base that supplanted the farmland; but they preferred the World War II Army air field base over my university, which now runs roughshod over the place. In short, human development has been pretty hard on the burrowing owls.

My university has cultivated a long and ambivalent relationship with our owls, which preceded our occupancy. A burrowing owl is our mascot—his name is Owlsley—and we've paid a "rebranding" outfit upwards of $30,000 to transform this friendly, peaceable fellow into an ornery, fighting owl. Our concrete gymnasium is called The Burrow. "When Owlsley isn't chilling at The Burrow," his FAU website declares, "he is out in the community showing his Owl Pride." Our faculty and staff giving society, which raises funds for FAU, is called the Owl's Nest. Official university stationery (e.g., invitations, holiday cards, greetings from our President, and the like) features photographs and drawings of burrowing owls. If the birds happen to nest in an inconvenient place, we mark it off with stakes and bright ribbon and try to accommodate them over the short term, as state law requires. All the same, we continue to encroach upon their territory (and the gopher tortoise's territory, and the turf of countless flora) to build up the university with classroom buildings, parking lots, dormitories, and our new football stadium, squeezing the owls' actual burrows into ever-dwindling, overcrowded plots. The thousands of spectators who now attend our weekend football games probably take little notice of the flat field just to the north. Those who do take note of its existence may wonder why the university hasn't paved over this "empty" space to offer more convenient game-time parking; they may not recognize the significance of the two dozen or so low-lying, t-shaped perches, just yards from one another. Complicating matters for the burrowing owls, the feral cats that roam our campus do recognize these markers and have been known to decimate entire nests before the young can fledge.

I never know quite how to feel when I visit this concentrated plot of burrowing-owl nests. There's something exciting about seeing so many of these special owls, perched above their burrows on those roosts, or hunkered down on the dirt. Often, I'll see them swoop and glide on wings that seem longer and broader than you'd expect a bird their size to sport. I've told several new colleagues about this precious patch of real estate, often after they complain that they haven't yet seen one of our burrowing owls. I usually receive enthusiastic reports back from them on their successful sightings. Yet, as nice as it is to see these owls and point them out to new friends, as proud as I truly am that our owl mascot actually lives on our campus (I'm pretty sure that Temple University in Philadelphia, which also boasts an owl mascot, can't make the same claim), there's something depressing about gazing across at the diminished habitat that we offer our burrowing owls in the shadow of our new football stadium. They certainly wouldn't choose to live in such concentrated quarters if an option still existed. So they just do the best they can. A feeling of not-quite-rightness sits uneasily with my excitement as I spot one of these spunky raptors through my binoculars. We really haven't treated the burrowing owl particularly well, either at my university or throughout the rest of their U.S. range.

It may be that the burrowing owls' subterranean predilections accounts, in part, for our limited sympathy with them. Perhaps it's not any way for a self-respecting owl to behave. Even Willa Cather offers a somewhat equivocal appraisal of Nebraska's burrowing owls for this reason. "Sometimes," declares Jim Burden, the narrator of *My Ántonia* (1918), "I rode north to the big prairie-dog town, to watch the brown earth-owls fly home in the late afternoon and go down to their nests underground with the dogs." Jim and his friend, Ántonia Shimerda, feel sorry for the owls, which frequently lose their burrows and their eggs to the rattlesnakes. Yet they don't feel as sorry for the owls as one might expect. "It was always mournful to see them come flying home at sunset and disappear under the earth," Jim reflects. "But, after all, we felt, winged things who would live like that must be rather degraded creatures." Between the cornfields gaining increasing purchase westward across the plains and the burrowing owls, Cather, it must be said, cast her lot with the cornfields.

When I first moved to south Florida, I was immediately taken with these lovely little owls. Given the bustle of our increasingly metropolitan area, it seemed incredible to me—and still seems incredible—that these fierce little birds still lived among us, fighting the good fight. By contrast, and in fairness to Cather, it probably seemed unfathomable to her that her pioneers' cornfields, and suburban development, would ever replace 98 percent of her region's native tallgrass prairie, supplanting so many burrowing owls, snakes, and prairie dogs in the bargain. I wanted to learn more about these birds.

Most curiously, I discovered, burrowing owls, unlike other owls, are most active during the day, which is when they hunt. They have fairly eclectic alimentary interests and tend to eat small mammals, including moles, mice, voles, gophers, and even bats, during the late spring and early summer, before switching mostly to insects and other bugs, including grasshoppers, moths, crickets, beetles, and even scorpions. They also prey upon reptiles, amphibians, and other birds, ranging from horned larks to doves. They use a variety of strategies to hunt: walking and running across the ground for prey, swooping down from a hover or perch, and even capturing insects in flight, like flycatchers. The breeding season extends from March to late August, typically, and females lay six to twelve eggs that are incubated for twenty-eight to thirty days. Here's a fun fact: burrowing owls have been known to "decorate" the entrances to their nests with dung from cows, horses, and dogs, possibly to mask nest odors and avoid predation. The female does all the incubation and brooding, while her mate provides all the food. Owlets have a very interesting defense mechanism to ward off feral cats and other predators. When threatened, they emit a sound that emulates a rattlesnake. If they manage to survive, the young fledge at six weeks or so.

Burrowing owls have a somewhat broader range than I originally suspected and comprise two non-overlapping breeding populations: a western group that includes terrain from the Mississippi to the Pacific, and a Florida population. The plumage of our Florida birds is a bit darker. Despite the fairly broad range, and their opportunistic eating habits, the owls are in decline across all of their historic territory, according to The Burrowing Owl Conservation Network, based in California. Recent trend data suggests that fewer than ten thousand breeding pairs remain. Habitat destruction, caused primarily by land development (e.g., football fields) and prairie-dog control measures (i.e., chemical rodenticides), represent the greatest threat to the burrowing owls. They are listed as Endangered in Canada and Threatened in Mexico; considered a Bird of Conservation Concern by the U.S. Fish and Wildlife Service; and, at the state level, listed as Endangered in Minnesota, as Threatened in Colorado, as a Species of Concern in Arizona, California, Montana, Oklahoma, Oregon, Utah, Washington, and Wyoming, and as a Species of Special Concern in Florida.

I snapped off hundreds of photos of the owls my first few years here, skulking on my stomach as close as I could get to their burrows without frightening them. But I couldn't quite seem to get close enough to capture a good photo at their nest, or capture a shot of one of the creatures elsewhere without the "hand of man," as photographers say, contaminating the field of view. They'd perch on a chain-link fence, or on the man-made metal perch beside their burrow, shaped like a T, or one of our ugly concrete buildings would contaminate the backdrop. I cursed them for their recalcitrance on more than one occasion, my eyes stinging with sweat. It peeved me that they just wouldn't cooperate with my plans.

In retrospect, I wonder whether there's something emblematic about my early difficulties with the burrowing owls. I wonder whether my almost comical impatience with them typifies our relationship with the natural world, generally. We instinctively appreciate the realm of nonhuman nature, but only, I fear, on our own terms. Owls may be pretty to look at, but we're quick to call them a nuisance if their burrows get in the way of our plans. We're incredibly good at rationalizing our actions, too. After all, what self-respecting winged creature would burrow in the earth? Cather's Jim reflects. And so we've all but shoved the burrowing owls into a tiny corner of their range. Was my perspective on the owls so different? Here I was, cursing them that they wouldn't cooperate with my own efforts to capture them in a photograph so that I might decorate my office with a pretty picture.

I finally threw up my hands and framed my photo of a burrowing owl perched on a wooden survey marker, a diaphanous pink ribbon billowing in the wind beneath its talons. I hung the photo in my office and took a step back, taking it in, wishing that that stupid wooden survey marker wasn't there. But I like the photo now. It's more true, I think, than a photo I might have managed to capture without that wooden survey marker and its pink ribbon in the frame.

Here was a burrowing owl, a burrowing owl in Florida, struggling to hold on in spite of us, circa 2000.

9

Heat

"When Miami was awarded an NBA franchise to begin play in 1988, team officials wanted to have the fans in South Florida involved in the naming, so a contest was held. . . . Among more than 5,000 entries submitted were Sharks, Barracudas, Flamingos, Palm Trees, Beaches, Heat, Suntan, Shade, Tornadoes and Floridians. . . . 'The Heat was it,' said the team's general partner, Zev Bufman. 'When you think of Miami, that's what you think of.'"

NBA.COM

"IT'S LIKE STEPPING INTO SOMEONE'S MOUTH." So I was warned about the oppressive Florida heat by one of my new colleagues. It was 1996 and I had just moved to the subtropics from the more temperate Pennsylvania. These words occur to me now as we embark upon our second straight week of record-high October temperatures down here in the Sunshine State. Upper-90s. Heat index above 100. "Close," as long-in-the-tooth southerners refer to our hottest heat, which made sense to me only after I'd weathered a few south Florida summers. Unlike the dry heat in Los Angeles, where I was raised, the wet heat in south Florida envelops you, oozes into your very pores, truly offers you no space, but paints the whole canvas of your flesh with its scalding brush. To live here is to feel one way or another about this most salient feature of the state. Indifference isn't an option.

"I'm learning all about heat," my nine-year-old daughter, Sophia, tells me after I complain about this sweltering October (!) morning on our walk to school.

"What *is* heat, then?" I ask.

"Energy," she replies.

"Wow, interesting. I didn't know that."

"Duh, dad," my son, Henry, chimes in.

I decide to learn a bit more about the physical properties of heat, if only to wipe the smirk off of my son's face. "Heat is a form of energy and can be measured in units of mechanics, e.g., joules," the authors of *Elements of Physics* (1978) declare. But it took some time for scientists to reach this understanding. "Heat was considered a mysterious fluid" up until the cusp of the nineteenth century, Milton Rothman writes in *The Laws of Physics* (1963), one of several mysterious forces that "seemed to have no connection with kinetic or potential energy." Then, the German physicist Thomas Johann Seebeck demonstrated in 1822 that heat applied to the junction between two different metals could produce an electric current directly. A few years later, scientists would successfully reverse this experiment, demonstrating that electrical currents could produce heat or cold. By the mid-1800s, the British scientist James Prescott Joule (whence the name for units of heat measurement) measured the amount of heat obtained from a given unit of mechanical energy, proving that mechanical work could be converted into heat without loss and thereby inspiring the conservation of energy theory.

I can't really get these theoretical principles very close to me. In any case, it's the cultural force of heat, rather than its scientific properties, that most interests me. The extreme heat of Florida is the predominant factor that has rendered the state forbidding and alienating to many Americans. To summon Nature in the mind's eye, for most of us, still means to summon a temperate forest, stream, or mountain. It's no accident that our first national parks were established well west of the Mississippi (e.g., Yellowstone, Sequoia, Yosemite, Mount Rainier, Mesa Verde, Crater Lake), rather than in the broiling Everglades. Having cleared practically all the old-growth deciduous and coniferous forests east of the Appalachians by the end of the nineteenth century, our nation was ready to preserve any remaining places (patches of such places, anyway) that approximated these despoiled acres. And so the nation looked westward. John Muir, the greatest champion of the Sierras, could rely upon empathetic, temperate sensibilities when he described for these readers the splendor of Yosemite in his most popular work, *My First Summer in the Sierra* (1911). His writing proved instrumental in securing national-park status for Yosemite and also persuaded scores of easterners to visit the Sierras by train and, later, by car. His persuasiveness rested not so much in convincing readers of the strangeness of the Sierras as of their familiarity. The wild places out west were very much like the once-wild places out east, *only more so.* Taller trees, bigger mountains, deeper canyons, mightier rivers—but trees, mountains, canyons, and rivers, all the same.

South Florida in the late nineteenth and early twentieth centuries, by contrast, must have seemed an utterly alien wilderness to most newcomers—an unbearably hot, mosquito-infested wasteland, not so much to be preserved or appreciated as redeemed. Governor Napoleon Broward, for whom we've named our second-most populous county, sought with ruthless abandon to dredge as much of the swamp as he could. He pursued this agenda under the banner of conservation. To save the Everglades, for Broward and most other "conservationists" during the first decades of the twentieth century, was not only to keep railroads and other corporate interests out (a good thing, surely) but also to "reclaim" the swamp by draining it, transforming it into farmland. "The Everglades should be saved," Broward declares in his 1905 inaugural address, and continues without ironic intent, "They should be drained and made fit for cultivation."

Small wonder that advocates for preserving the Everglades as a national park would have a much tougher time of it than Muir did. The origins of the campaign can be traced to an influential group of Florida women, among them May Mann Jennings, the wife of a former Florida governor, who dedicated four thousand acres of Royal Palm State Park in 1916—a relatively small parcel at the heart of the current Everglades National Park. Inspired by the efforts of Jennings and her allies, Ernest Coe, David Fairchild, Marjory Stoneman Douglas, and others would labor for decades to convince Congress and the public, not least of all fellow Floridians, that the forbidding environment of the Everglades was worthy of preservation rather than reclamation.

Heat. The Everglades originate in the sun's heat, Douglas recognizes in her classic work, *The Everglades: River of Grass* (1947). "When the original saw grass thrust up its spears into the sun," Douglas writes, "the fierce sun, lord and power and first cause over the Everglades as of all the green world, then the Everglades began." Douglas appreciated, better than anyone at the time, that the entire biota of the subtropics, flora and fauna, didn't exist in spite of the fierce heat but because of it. "There must be heat and wetness," she observes, "for the porous thirty or more eggs the female alligator lays. . . . It may take eight weeks or more, with the sun heat and the ferment and the moisture, to incubate them." All the same, Douglas was wary of the unrelenting nature of the Florida heat when it came to our human endeavors. She wasn't much of an outdoorswoman, actually. She appreciated wild Florida, and sought to preserve it as fiercely as anyone ever would, but she was content to leave it be, living most of her rich and abundant life in Miami proper in her (non-air-conditioned) Coconut Grove cottage. "To try to make one's way among these impenetrable tufts," she writes in *The Everglades: River of Grass* of the seemingly interminable stretches of sawgrass, "is to be cut off from all air, to be beaten down by the sun and ripped by the grassy saw-toothed edges as one sinks in mud and water over the roots." She would later remark, "To be a friend of the Everglades is not necessarily to spend time wandering around out there. . . . It's too buggy, too wet, too generally inhospitable." It's an offhand observation, but I find something incredibly humble, and admirable, about its implications. Douglas was able to think about the natural world and our relationship to it in a way that wasn't at all prevalent during her time, or even ours. Nature ought to be preserved, regardless of whether it could be put to our commercial or recreational use. This was the philosophical leap necessary even to begin thinking about granting the Everglades the status of National Park and its associated protections.

The park would not gain its status until 1947, and within much smaller boundaries than an embittered Coe had in mind. In his dedication speech for Everglades National Park, President Truman strikes a defensive chord, acknowledging the more familiar western version of nature and the comparatively alien quality of Florida's unconstructed landscape: "Here are no lofty peaks seeking the sky, no mighty glaciers or rushing streams wearing away the uplifted land. Here is land, tranquil in its quiet beauty, serving not as the source of water but as the last receiver of it." If Muir's triumph was to convince the public that the Sierras were a majestic wilderness worth preserving so that we might experience it, advocates for the Everglades—an "irreplaceable primitive area," according to Truman—would triumph by convincing Washington that its ecosystem was worth preserving, even if most Americans would rather spend their leisure time elsewhere.

Everglades National Park was the only national park that Ansel Adams never visited and photographed during his lifetime.

Despite the heat, humans did, and do, live in the Everglades. And so shelter, for Florida's Native Americans, has meant something different than what shelter means for many Americans. The idea isn't so much to keep the heat in as to let it out. The Seminole and Miccosukee taught themselves how to build ventilated shelters relatively recently, as their ancestors were not native to the state. (Spanish conquistadors had eradicated the native Timucuan, Apalachee, Calusa, and other Florida tribes by the end of the eighteenth century.) The Seminole and Miccosukee migrated to Florida from their native Alabama and Georgia terrain in significant numbers only by the 1800s, either raiding Spanish encampments or, mostly, fleeing from hostile white encroachment on their territory. These Native Americans in northern Florida built Creek housing structures, log cabins, essentially. William Bartram describes several of these villages, and his amicable reception by the Native Americans, in *Travels* (1791). While the Native Americans in northern Florida apparently enjoyed good relations with the British during their brief rule of the peninsula, the United States under Andrew Jackson initiated what can only be described as an extirpation campaign against the Native Americans living in Florida (three "Seminole" Wars), forcing the increasingly scattered tribes further down to the peninsula's toe-tip, below Lake Okeechobee, deeper into the subtropical muck and heat. The Everglades heat must have seemed to them a strange and powerful force.

Seminole and Miccosukee architecture would evolve to address the broiling climate of south Florida. Jettisoning the dark, enclosed Creek structures, which acted like convection ovens, the Native Americans invented the "chickee," an open-sided dwelling framed by bald cypress logs and roofed with intricate palmetto thatching. A wooden platform three feet or so off the ground provided a dry living space and protection from snakes and other varmints. Many early white observers recognized the dwellings as works of art. Chickees have demonstrated amazing durability throughout the years, the thatched roofs repelling the most torrential downpours and the open frame offering cross-ventilation galore and, even more importantly, permitting the safe passage of hurricane-force winds.

The white Florida settlers from 1840 to 1920, or thereabouts, built slightly more elaborate homes, called Cracker homes. These domiciles, like the chickees, were built from local materials and designed to address the special ecological pressures of Florida. Early Cracker homes were one-story cedar or cypress cabins, raised off the hot, moist, snake-infested ground with oyster shell or lime pilings. Wide porches and numerous windows offered cross-ventilation and relief from the sun, while steep metal roofs warded off Florida's torrential downpours. Stone or block chimneys allowed the white settlers, or Crackers, to build fires for heat during occasional cold winter days.

A robust market exists today among restaurants, parks, and private home-owners for chickee patios, bars, and simple shelters. A famous old restaurant just up the road from me in Lantana, the Old Key Lime House, boasts that their enormous chickee patio withstood our recent hurricanes with hardly a displaced palm frond. Chickees are prevalent enough in our state to have earned a separate "Chickee Hut Permit Application" in the Florida Building Code.

The demand for chickee "huts"—a redundancy as the word *chickee* means *home* in the languages spoken by the Seminole and Miccosukee—provides a good source of labor for Seminole and Miccosukee craftsmen. Yet we don't appreciate chickees for what they once were, and still are for some Native Americans living in the Everglades. We erect them mostly in the spirit of Florida kitsch. But chickees, and Cracker houses, do everything that a home ought to do. They provide shelter suited organically to the local environment, so organically in the case of the chickee that these Native American villages in the Everglades blend into the local environment, making them difficult for outsiders to detect.

We don't build homes any more suited to the heat of the subtropics. We haven't needed to do so. John Gorrie, sometime in the 1830s, built an air conditioner (or, at least, something approximating an air conditioner) in Apalachicola, Florida. To alleviate the suffering of his yellow fever and malaria patients in our hot state, Dr. Gorrie's machine deposited ice in a bucket and channeled a current of air over it to cool the hospital room. Willis Carrier, an engineer at the Buffalo Forge Company, would become the father of modern air conditioning by inventing the more efficient "Apparatus for Treating Air" in 1906, for which he received U.S. patent #808897. The system of chilled coils represented a breakthrough as it not only cooled the air but also lowered the humidity to 55 percent. Additional breakthroughs by Carrier and others continued over the next several years, and air conditioning spread from commercial to residential use. Individual, window-installed air-conditioning units had become widespread in southern homes by the 1950s, and Florida's population boom was upon us.

South Florida only emerged as a viable place for widespread year-round habitation, then, once we were able to manufacture and import the temperate climate of the Northeast, which, in turn, allowed us to forgo the chickee and the Cracker home in favor of the ecologically nonsensical, heat-absorbing concrete and stucco houses that mostly grace our subdivisions today. In this way, the subdivisions of south Florida approximate the homogenous, faux-

Mediterranean concrete and stucco developments throughout practically every outpost of America's suburbia.

One might view heat and its associated mosquitoes as Florida's greatest environmentalists; they kept human encroachment in the state at bay for years.

Florida Power & Light (FPL), the largest electric utility company in the state, serving 4.5 million accounts, contends that weather (i.e., air conditioning and heating) accounts for the largest portion of its consumers' electric bills. Florida homeowners average well over 1,000 kilowatt hours (kwh) of electricity consumption per year. While FPL forecasts a lower load growth in its most recent Ten Year Power Plant Site Plan, the behemoth for-profit company still projects a substantial total growth. Summer peak electricity usage, when Floridians crank up the air, is projected to increase to 26,143 megawatts (mw) by 2018, an increase of 5,066 mw over the 2008 actual summer peak.

FPL currently obtains its power from multiple sources: 52 percent natural gas, 19 percent nuclear, 15 percent purchased, 8 percent oil, 6 percent coal. To address Florida's randy demand for electricity, FPL's Ten Year Power Plant Site Plan includes ramping up the power production at their current nuclear facilities at Turkey Point and St. Lucie and constructing additional natural gas–fired combined-cycle generating units at proposed sites throughout the state. Compared to oil and coal, natural gas burns cleaner and produces energy more efficiently through combined-cycle technology (i.e., gas and steam turbines). Natural gas remains a carbon-based fossil fuel and produces planet-warming carbon dioxide, all the same.

Floridians have worried about the antisocial ramifications of Carrier's cooling apparatus from the get-go. A professor at the University of South Florida, Raymond Arsenault, famously warned, "General Electric has proved a more devastating invader than General Sherman." What Arsenault feared was that our self-imposed isolation, facilitated in large part by air conditioning, would erode our sense of community and even basic civility—hallmarks of the Southern ethos. It's a tough argument to dispute from my current vantage. It's fair to say, I think, that most of us don't so much *live* in the subtropical heat as evade it altogether. One might be tempted to say that we treat summers sort of as our counterparts in the Northeast treat winters. I've lived in both places, however, and I would argue that our aversion to the extreme heat in Florida, and the lengths to which we go to avoid it, far exceeds the reaction of most northeasterners to the cold. The dailiness of south Florida life during the wet season approximates a science-fiction novel set on a hostile, alien planet. We might not wear special space suits, but we mostly seal ourselves hermetically against the outside, and against one another, for months at a time in climate-controlled interiors (homes, offices, cars). Few people wile away the time on Cracker-style front porches in my hometown. Try finding front porches in my neighborhood!

It would be good if we, if I, could learn to love the Florida heat, not unlike the way that we learn to love (if we're lucky) those most impossible qualities of our children and spouses. To be a Floridian, I've come to believe—not just someone who lives in Florida, but a true Floridian—is to welcome the state's hottest months as well as its more temperate months.

Books offer little encouragement. Heat in our western literature—now I'm talking about heat here, not warmth—has long been associated with danger, racially laced barbarousness, and sexual licentiousness. This pernicious literary symbolism manifests itself in too many literary examples to enumerate, but one might begin by contemplating the bible and biblically inspired works (e.g., Milton's *Paradise Lost,* Dante's *Inferno*) and read straight through to Joseph Conrad's *Heart of Darkness* and beyond.

It takes a Florida writer, maybe, to know heat and to write heat, which is to know and evoke its literal rather than symbolic significance, and in appreciative terms. And so let us contemplate the work of a largely neglected writer, Marjorie Kinnan Rawlings, who in 1928 moved from America's snowbelt to Florida's woolly interior to run an orchard, and to write. She would win a Pulitzer Prize for *The Yearling* (1938), but her less well-known memoir, *Cross Creek* (1942), represents an even finer literary accomplishment, I think. While Rawlings' profiles of her colorful Florida neighbors take up much of the memoir, some of my favorite sections of the book involve Rawlings' close evocations of the wild land itself. Her descriptions of summer heat in Florida strike me as particularly knowing and fine, not least of all because Rawlings—unimprisoned by air conditioning—followed the encouragement of our wet season to live more slowly and to watch the workings of nature more deliberately. "Folk who have never known a tropical summer have never luxuriated in indolence. . . . I have lain on my veranda and asked no more of the summer day than to watch, one by one, the lotus petals falling." Such careful watching accounts for her tactile, reverent rendering of Florida's heat. Rawlings experiences heat fully in *Cross Creek*, and writes heat fully, tapping all the senses. There's something palpably alive and organic about heat in her writing. It never simply *is*, but *does*. During its most apparently inert, oppressive moments, heat's busy gaining momentum, gathering its breath to stir the palm fronds and Spanish moss in advance of the rain. That Rawlings knows heat intimately, including all of its associated phenomena, accounts for her sympathies. Even the most miserable moments in the Florida heat seem laced with something close to affection in Rawlings' memoir. She never curses the heat outright. Rather, she touches its many sides. One cannot experience the rainbow or the rosy light of a summer evening without the earlier stifling heat of the summer day.

Don't give up on the outdoors, I say, even during Florida's hottest heat. To experience these months with something close to alacrity, it's best to limit your exposure to air conditioning. The heat doesn't seem so hot if you don't shutter yourself away in the cold. When driving, open the windows, jut out your left arm and splay your fingers to court the warm currents. Don't give up on the outdoors. Walk outside, but walk slowly. It took me a long time to recognize that if I just slowed my brisk pace, I could walk outdoors in the dead of summer without succumbing to nausea. Drink water. Drink more water. Apply sunscreen liberally to your exposed flesh, whatever your pigmentation. Appreciate the physiological role that sweat plays in a subtropical life. Fear not those half-moons that erupt beneath your armpits on your shirt sleeves. Fear not the faintest trace of your human smell. Purchase a light, broad-brimmed hat, and wear it. Purchase large polarized sunglasses, and wear them. Don't give up on the outdoors.

There's something awe-inspiring about the Florida heat, which I've slowly learned to appreciate. Its relentless, inexorable force. I'll stand outside in the middle of a scalding day sometimes, close my eyes, and lift my face, just to feel the sheer power of the sun's heat against my flesh, and I'm put in my place. I feel very small during these moments, which isn't a bad way to feel sometimes. My problems tend to feel smaller too. The world, I realize during these brief moments, was not designed for us. At least not for us alone, despite what our traditions may tell us. This earth is far more terrific than the meager version of it that we've tamed and cultivated for our use, and it's more terrifying too. We ought to mind our manners during our brief time here.

It's not always easy to love the heat. "We're moving to Baltimore," a close friend told me a few months ago, during the middle of our scalding summer. "I got a great job up there, and it's too darn hot down here." We've suffered more than our share of these small abandonments over the years. American life is increasingly transitory, and Florida is one of our most transitory states, partly on account of its unrelenting heat. Not everyone can take it. I hated the heat when my friend told me that they were moving. I felt like the speaker of Wallace Stevens' "Farewell to Florida," who resents the Florida heat and its associates—the "bleaching sand," the "vivid blooms," the "trees like bones"—upon the termination of one of his human relationships in the state. It's not always easy to love the heat.

Still, there's so much about Florida that I love, much of which I've described in this book. I've dug myself in here and I'm determined to make a go of it. I take heart in the creatures, human and nonhuman, who've dug in for far longer than I have. Like gopher tortoises and burrowing owls, who dig in, literally, dodging the heat. It's a strange way for tortoises and owls to go about their life business, but it's a way that works. The Seminole and Miccosukee and Crackers, too, invented a completely new version of home to endure and thrive in the subtropical heat and muck. My own efforts seem paltry, by contrast. Hardly efforts at all. I won't even forgo air conditioning, completely. Yet I've resolved to build a chickee with Henry and Sophia, if only to take its measure, and for the fresh vantage point it might provide on my shelter, proper.

I've done the reading, which is typically my first step before doing anything. To build a chickee, more or less according to basic specifications, start with the frame. Cypress wood if you can find it. Other hardwoods, pines, or even palm tree trunks will do. Plant your four poles at the desired dimensions. Square or rectangle. Build your roof frame. Attach struts, boards, or small diameter trees from the length of the top of each pole to the center of the chickee. Strut length determines roof pitch. Place crossbeams on the struts in preparation for palm-frond thatching. Six inches apart for saw palmetto; twelve inches apart for cabbage palmetto. Build your platform. Milled wood works fine. The higher the platform, the less heat radiates from the earth to the living surface. On to the thatching. Collect palm fronds first. Broader fronds work best. Cut leaves from the base of the trunk with a machete. Cut fronds to a stem length of four to five feet. Stack and dry for forty-eight hours or so. Place each frond on the crossbeam, flat side of the stem down. Tie fronds to crossbeams with sawgrass, rushes, or palm-frond fingers. Overlap fronds as you go. Tight weave for a waterproof roof.

Don't give up on the outdoors.

10

Snail Kite

THE SNAIL KITE (*ROSTRHAMUS SOCIABILIS*), also known as the Everglades kite, tries my patience. It stubbornly refuses to live in the real world, to adapt and overcome like the rest of us. In short, it eats pretty much one thing and one thing only, the apple snail. That it's critically endangered in its south Florida range—with only a few hundred breeding pairs or so holding on—seems comeuppance for its intractable dietary fussiness. At least this is how I feel in my most stingy, unfair moods, fearful as I am over the potentially bleak future of snail kites in my state.

When I moved to Florida, the snail kite was at the top of the list of birds I wanted to see. Who knew how much longer anyone would have to see this raptor beating its wings above the Everglades, scanning the shallow river of sawgrass below for the shimmer of phantom apple snails? Between my domestic and workplace obligations, I set about finding snail kites, casually with my wife, but in greater earnest with my birding friend, Rob, during his intermittent visits from Pennsylvania. We memorized their features so that we'd know them at a glimpse and not confuse them with northern harriers. "All black except for a broad white band across the base of its tail; legs red," Roger Tory Peterson claims in *A Field Guide to the Birds* (1934). His illustration beside his description reveals an ostentatiously long and curved bill, unlike any raptor's bill I'd ever seen. Rob and I tried spotting the birds countless times at the Arthur R. Marshall Loxahatchee National Wildlife Refuge in Boynton Beach, the northernmost remnant of the Everglades, a nearly 150,000-acre green thumbprint hemmed in between the "Everglades Agricultural Area" around Lake Okeechobee and rampant residential and commercial development to the east. No dice. While we frequently observed small flocks of the rare smooth-billed anis (something like a grackle, but with a swollen, bulbous bill), the snail kites eluded us. We began taking longer day trips westward along the Tamiami Trail, a concrete and asphalt scar across the abdomen of the natural Everglades demarcating the northern boundary of the human-designated Everglades National Park today. Completed in 1928, the Tamiami Trail, as its name suggests, was the first highway linking Tampa to Miami and, more generally, southeast Florida to the Gulf coast. The larger highway across southern Florida, Alligator Alley, would open just north of the Tamiami Trail in 1968. Unfortunately, the Tamiami Trail and its adjacent canal have acted as a dam to the southward flowing river of grass, choking off the natural water flow and devastating the ecology. Integral to the Comprehensive Everglades Restoration Plan, or CERP—the precise details of which various parties have been wrangling over since 2000—are proposals to build a bridge over an extended section of the Tamiami Trail to partially restore the natural water flow from Lake Okeechobee to the Florida Bay.

On several weekends, Rob and I drove along the small, congested highway, our eyes peeled north and south for hovering snail kites but seeing only cheesy shops and stands seeking to capitalize upon tourists' apparent affinity for alligators, Native American kitsch, sea shells, and citrus. We stopped at Shark Valley on a few occasions, a fifteen-mile paved loop jutting south from the Tamiami Trail into the Everglades. It's one of the few locales that the American Birding Association's *A Birder's Guide to Florida* (1996) highlighted for snail kites. You know a species is in trouble when experts start identifying the *one* place, or few places, where it might be seen. On each of our trips, we meandered a few miles down the loop, our binoculars at the ready. We didn't see any snail kites but managed, once, to see an enormous wild boar rooting around the brittle, dry-season brush, just twenty feet or so off the paved road. We reported the sighting and location to a young ranger, who told us that he'd have to "put a cap in him." The boars, introduced to Florida by the first Spanish Conquistadors, are apparently doing quite a bit of damage to the Everglades flora with their ferocious foraging.

Rob and I finally spotted our snail kites in March 1999, two of them on the north side of Tamiami Trail, a mile or so west of the Shark Valley entrance. "Jeez, is that them?" I exclaimed, pointing out my open window toward the two raptors beating their wings above the sawgrass. Rob swerved treacherously toward the berm and nearly skidded to a stop, inspiring a chorus of car horns behind us. We spilled out of the car and gazed at the raptors for several minutes, neither Rob nor I speaking a word. The birds cooperated by working a patch of sawgrass within binocular range for several minutes. Every once in a while one of the birds would fold its wings some and list in the air, diving down toward prospective snail-prey, I imagined, only to correct itself, gaining altitude once again. They struck me as much lovelier than Peterson's drawings suggested, their plumage more graphite gray than black, their legs and cere (the fleshy swelling on the bills of some birds) more orange than red.

"That's definitely them," Rob finally intoned, without lowering his binoculars.

Here these snail kites were, doing what snail kites do. They seemed utterly outside the confusions of our world, but, of course, they were utterly at the mercy of our caprice, as well. For here I was, standing on an asphalt berm gazing beyond a concrete-lined canal at these birds hoping to locate suitable prey north of the Tamiami Trail, once the Everglades proper, but now a "Water Conservation Area." Over the course of the past hundred years or so—the years since Governor Napoleon Broward set about "redeeming" the Everglades by dredging them—we had utterly changed the ground rules for any animal hoping to survive in south Florida. One hundred years. A mere blip on the screen of the snail kite (and human) story. How impoverished and churlish was my former take on these birds, it occurred to me. Developing a yen for apple snails wasn't fussy at all but an incredibly savvy, adaptive move for these raptors. Eating escargot served the snail kite incredibly well for thousands and thousands of years, allowing it to escape the competition over more common raptor prey.

Several years would pass before I'd see snail kites again. In the summer of 2008, several snail-kite pairs set up housekeeping in the C-8 impoundment right off the heavily trammeled marsh trail at Loxahatchee. It didn't take long for word to spread over the Internet. I rushed to the refuge with Henry and Sophia and after a short walk down the trail, spotted several of the adult birds on and near their nests in the low-lying cypress trees. A surfeit of snail kites! Good news, it would appear, but maybe not such good news. Rangers at the refuge and expert birders on scene thought that the snail kites' breeding efforts here in this managed section of the refuge just off the highway most likely reflected the growing deterioration of their more preferred nesting habitat in the Everglades proper, just beyond the levee a half-mile or so to our west. It's still not clear whether their breeding efforts in the C-8 impoundment were successful, in any case. A local owl, apparently, ate several of the chicks.

We should preserve and restore the critical snail-kite habitat that we have mostly destroyed. We should do so for the simple sake of snail kite-ness in the world. We can value snail kites on their own terms, however, while still extracting something useful for ourselves in their story. I think of all that transpired across Florida's human realm of affairs in the nearly ten-year span between my first sighting of snail kites and my second sighting in the summer of 2008: Elian Gonzales, butterfly ballots, anthrax, Terri Schiavo, Mark Foley, the Space Shuttle Columbia disaster, the housing bubble and its bursting. Human life moves so impossibly fast. I think of the dizzying pace of my own professional life over those ten years, scrapping feverishly to add lines to my curriculum vitae. All this time the embattled snail kites labored only to go about their most essential snail-kite business, against the increasingly bad hand that we've mostly dealt them. My wife and I conducted essential business too during this ten-year span, raising two fledglings of our own. But I'm not sure we did so as deliberately and mindfully as the snail kite, distracted as we both were by the extraneous confusions of our harried culture. Parenting is hard. Everyone knows this, of course, and so maybe it's a silly thing to say. But it's harder than I ever thought it would be. And parents receive very little encouragement outside the domestic sphere, whatever politicos might claim about our "family-values" culture. We would do better—as individuals and as a society—to raise our young by earnest, hopeful, and tireless snail-kite standards.

The Tale of a Cuban Immigrant

I RECEIVED THE TERSE DIRECTIVE from my friend Rob over e-mail, "Furman, find this bird!" Below the single admonitory line, he pasted the Florida rare-bird-alert posting he had just discovered on the Internet:

> 10/30 A CUBAN PEWEE has been seen the past two mornings (10/29 & 30) about 11:00 a.m. at the Gumbo Limbo Nature Center on A1A in Boca Raton. The bird was heard calling this morning, 10/30. The location of the park is approximately 1 mile south of Spanish River Blvd. on A1A. The park has restrictive hours and is open on Sunday from 12 noon to 4 p.m. and Mon. through Saturday 9 a.m. to 4:00 p.m. Parking is non-existent on A1A and it is not advisable to go any other time than park hours.

I canceled my morning office hours at the university, grabbed my binoculars, stuffed my tattered copy of Roger Tory Peterson's *Eastern Birds* in my hip pocket, and made haste to Gumbo Limbo Park.

I shouldn't give the wrong impression. As far as birders go, I am no expert—just someone a bit north of novice. That is, I spend enough early mornings on the activity that students, friends, and family members tease me, but I am not so totally immersed in the avian realm that the most fervent birders don't strike me also as a bit odd. I run into these birding aficionados often in Florida, the ones who travel in hordes from faraway states for the mere chance to glimpse a colorful straggler from the tropics: a stripe-headed tanager, a Key West quail dove, a bananaquit, or one of the countless others blown off course by the latest hurricane. I don't imagine I'll ever count myself among those who regularly consult various nationwide rare-bird alerts on the Internet and cash in their frequent flyer miles accordingly. All the same, no birder worth his or her salt in the United States would pass up the opportunity to see a Cuban pewee currently sharing the same zip code. Only once before, in 1995, has a Cuban-pewee sighting been confirmed in the United States, just a mile or so up the coastal highway (the A1A) from Gumbo Limbo Park, as a matter of fact. That particular bird proved to be a gregarious little thing. It flitted about Spanish River Park in Boca Raton for over a month and seemed nearly to pose for the camera-wielding birders who flew in on steel wings from all over the country to add the small, gray flycatcher to their North American life-list.

Given the hoopla over the last Cuban pewee, I wasn't surprised to encounter a host of eager birders along the short Nature Trail loop who had beaten me to Gumbo Limbo Park. In terms of sheer acreage, it's a modest little park, nestled on the barrier island between the Atlantic Ocean to the east and Florida's intracoastal waterway to the west, and bordered on the north and south by upscale high-rise condominiums. Yet the mantra of real-estate agents (location, location, location) crucially applies to this little patch of green. For these few surviving natural areas along the south Florida coast—densely wooded with the symmetrical leaves and sunburnt, peeling bark of the gumbo limbo, the sprawling muscular limbs of live oak, and the fragrant wax myrtle, along with strangler fig, firebush, ironwood, sabal palm, wild coffee, satinleaf, marlberry, and various non-native interlopers from the plant realm—are increasingly vital. Like, say, Central Park in New York, these isolated acres of flora provide temporary refuge for a concentrated number of birds migrating amid an otherwise inhospitable jungle of concrete and stucco.

It was early in the morning, so all the birders were fresh and at the top of their game. As if by silent agreement, they had fanned out in the small swath of woods and dense underbrush. A potential "lifer" in their midst, there was little time for socializing. Wanting to play my part, I staked out some vacant turf of my own and scanned the shrubbery for the telltale field marking of the Cuban pewee: half an eye-ring, a sliver of the moon on each side of its face. An aura of resolution permeated our little group. If this bird was still hanging around, we were going to see it. Having no luck with my binoculars, I concentrated on the sounds about me. The pewee had, evidently, been calling quite a bit—calling, it occurred sadly to me, in search of other Cuban pewees it stood little chance of finding in south Florida. The Cuban pewee's call, a rapid *pit-*

pit-pit-pit-pit, is distinct and, therefore, diagnostic. But all I could hear were the thin, wheezy notes of the tiny, prolific gnatcatchers, which were flitting about in the shrubs all around me, and the monotonous, exasperating automotive hum of the A1A to the east just beyond the narrow remnant of green. Gazing off toward the ocean, searching fiercely for our little Cuban immigrant, it was tough not to reflect upon the countless human immigrants from Cuba, tough not to draw an analogue in these few ounces of feathers and bones desperately flapping above the turbulent waters of the Florida Straits to reach our shore. How could one not brood upon the contrastive greetings we afford the human and avian immigrants from Cuba? Pepper spray for the human refugees (the current practice of the Coast Guard to prevent Cuban refugees from reaching the beach), a welcoming committee of awestruck citizens from across the country for the feathered immigrants. And, as I write these lines, the United States and Cuba wrangle perversely over the custody of a six-year-old Cuban child found bobbing in an inner tube off the Florida Coast on Thanksgiving Day.

Birding, generally speaking, offers ample opportunity for such extended reflection. It's one of the things I love about it—the rare encouragement it offers to this undervalued activity—and might partly account for its growing popularity among others, as well. The number of birding organizations, conferences, Internet sites, and publications grows at a staggering rate; the American Birding Association alone boasts nearly twenty thousand members. As I've suggested, our Zeitgeist hardly encourages such "idleness." The proliferation of e-mail, smartphones, and even upscale walkie-talkies ensure that we are ever on-call. I have managed to resist some of these technological marvels, but not all of them. Indeed, for me, birding serves as a respite from a life "frittered away by detail," I fear, beyond Thoreau's worst nightmares. As my working days increasingly fragment into ten-minute tasks—e-mail replies, telephone calls, student drop-bys—those extended stretches of time simply to sit and think that I had once so enjoyed have become all the more rare . . . and precious. In this sense, birding strikingly parallels two other precious activities in my life: reading and writing. All three activities, after all, require time, thought, and patience.

Still, on this particular morning at Gumbo Limbo Park, my patience was thinning in direct proportion to the number of scarlet mosquito bites that had begun to swell upon my calves and neck. Crisp early morning rapidly gave way to the heat of mid-morning in the subtropics. After studying the bushes for nearly two hours, we had all grown discouraged and suspended our vigilance to socialize a bit. I met various Floridians from throughout the state, a retired couple from New Jersey, and a stout, amiable mail carrier from Iowa who had found someone to cover his route and flew in that morning for his chance to see the Cuban pewee. His return flight departed later that afternoon and he was beginning somewhat desperately to estimate exactly how long it would take him to drive back to the Palm Beach International Airport. We all shuffled our feet in the rock and dirt trail, passed around bug repellant, compared notes on various birds we had recently seen, cross-checked the information we had individually received on this purported Cuban pewee sighting, and pondered our chances of spotting the rare bird before the daylight failed us.

The morning was not completely without excitement. One fellow managed to spot a rare short-tailed hawk, chocolate brown in its dark phase, perched high upon a droopy Australian pine limb overhanging the intracoastal waterway. A fellow birder was kind enough to retrieve his tripod and spotting scope from his car and focus it upon the raptor. We all took turns peering through the lens. Fewer than five hundred of these birds remain in the United States, all year-round residents of Florida, all struggling to survive across their ever dwindling North American niches of hardwood swamp, mixed pine forest, dry prairie, and marshland. Lamentably, the material interests of commercial, residential, and agricultural developers (read: Big Sugar) have long held sway over the short-tailed hawk's more modest ambitions. The hawk was a "lifer" for the couple who flew in from New Jersey. I had seen only one before, flying over the Tamiami Trail, the asphalt scar that runs all the way across Florida's shin and—as Marjory Stoneman Douglas presciently foresaw in *The Everglades: River of Grass* (1947)—has contributed to the devastation of the Everglades through choking the southerly flow of the river of grass. It had been a fleeting glimpse from this unfortunate highway, little more than a dipping off into the distant sawgrass. This was by far a better "look." I studied the bird carefully, seared its salient features into my brain: its chunky profile, its dark chocolate plumage, the black-and-white design of its tail band. If I'm lucky enough to see the short-tailed hawk again on our continent, I'll recognize it at a glance.

"Over here, over here!" a member of our cadre suddenly hissed from underneath a stand of Australian pines to the south, swaying in the breeze. In seconds, we had abandoned the scope and converged upon her.

"There, do you hear that?" she inquired. Yes, we all could hear it, an odd-sounding chirp, slightly nasal. Perhaps we had found our man! We all strained our necks to scan the droopy limbs and needles of the pines.

"No . . . no . . . false alarm," one of the men regretfully announced. "It's just a squirrel." Was he absolutely certain? someone asked desperately. It was such an odd sound for a squirrel to make, after all.

"Well," the fellow responded—his neck still craned back, his binoculars fixed at its location high above us in the canopy of dusty-green needles—"I can see the squirrel's mouth open, and then I hear the chirping." Fair enough. We all strode back mournfully to our stations.

By midday, we had grown weary. "Exactly *when* has it been spotted?" the Iowan inquired of me, as if my local residency somehow rendered more reliable the information I had received over the Internet like everyone else.

"My friend told me late morning," I answered, emphasizing the word late, hoping to bolster his spirits.

By one o'clock, the Iowan was sitting on a large rock, taking slow, sad bites of a sandwich he had prepared for himself that morning before heading for the airport. I sat down beside him. "I don't think I'm going to see it," he announced matter-of-factly. I felt bad for him. He had come all this way.

No, we probably weren't going to spot our Cuban pewee, I thought. And so I shifted strategies. Wordlessly, we all shifted strategies. As long as we were out there, we might as well take pleasure in the usual suspects. To be sure, the usual suspects along the southern coast of Florida in the fall are none too shabby. On purely aesthetic grounds, the warblers that migrate each year through our neighborhood on their way to their winter residences in South America are far more impressive than the Cuban pewee. We soon found ourselves in the middle of what birders call a "warbler wave." In the giant strangler fig before me, bereft of birds just a moment ago, I suddenly spotted various yellow fluttering within the glossy green leaves and could hear the determined *chipping* of various warblers over the din of the coastal highway. Before braving the long stretch of ocean between North and South America, they had stopped at Gumbo Limbo Park to gorge on Florida's countless variety of airborne insects, many of the same insects, no doubt, that had been gorging on me! In just a half-hour or so, we identified over ten warbler species rather actively paused at the southern tip of the United States. The park was ablaze with these tiny feathered sparks of color: the egg yolk on the throat of the yellow-throated, the cerulean crown and back of the black-throated blue, the bold black mustache against the rich yellow background of the prairie, the olive-green back and chestnut breast-band of the northern parula, the sunset orange and ebony black fan of the American redstart's tail, the faint milk-chocolate stain down the sides of a bay-breasted chest.

Suddenly, in the midst of this warbler wave, our single-minded pursuit of the Cuban pewee seemed vaguely mercenary to me. Mostly, whenever the opportunity arises I light out to various Florida outposts to observe the routine and proper workings of the natural world. The endeavor takes more and more strenuous effort these days in my part of the world, and probably in most parts of the industrialized world. Indeed, the indigenous rhythms throughout the state of Florida grow all the more faint; and, complicating matters, *we* grow increasingly deaf to them. These rhythms reverberate out of earshot as we cower in our climate-controlled cars, homes, and offices. How better to access this rhythm once again than to partake in the fiercely reliable annual migration of birds, to plunge headfirst into a warbler wave? If only, I reflected, the warblers weren't so diminutive, so relatively quiet. If only they weren't so downright unobtrusive during their stopover in south Florida. Would that a warbler wave could wash over our high-rises and homes to the north and south of the park and stir us all from our stupor.

In his landmark work, *Arctic Dreams* (1986), Barry Lopez sets out to capture the rhythm indigenous to the Arctic and recognizes the crucial role that migration plays in this unique ecosystem. "I came to think of the migrations as breath," Lopez reflects, "as the land breathing. In spring a great inhalation of light and animals. The long-bated breath of summer. And an exhalation that propelled them all south in the fall." Migration. The land breathing. To partake of these migrations, if only as a silent witness, is to feel the very breath of the land coursing through one's hair. Indeed, on an October day in Florida one can greet a bounty of birds blown southward by an Arctic exhale!

Looked at from one perspective, migration is a thoroughly complex, even inscrutable, natural phenomenon. Ornithologists continue to debate the why, when, where, and how of bird migration. Why does the buff-breasted sandpiper migrate so faithfully thousands and thousands of miles from its Arctic breeding ground to its winter home on the Argentinean Pampas when more northerly grasslands would appear to be available? How do pelagic birds navigate over vast stretches of nondescript ocean to reach their specific breeding grounds with such awe-inspiring punctuality? What, exactly, provokes the "pre-migratory restlessness"—the well-documented insomnia—that besets several species in the weeks and days just before they depart? Why, finally, don't the warblers in Gumbo Limbo Park simply remain in the tropics year-round, where they can dine on insects to their tiny heart's content, rather than undertake a perilous thousand-mile-plus journey twice a year? Competing theories abound regarding these and additional quandaries related to bird migration.

That said, migration might also be seen as the simplest of animal behaviors—as elemental as, yes, breathing. For the birds probably don't over think the how and the why of their peregrinations. They just go, spurred on by the inexorable command of instinct. "We're never single-minded, unperplexed, like migratory birds," the poet Rainer Maria Rilke observed. While there is much to be celebrated in the complexity of our human thoughts, how much I would give to feel the unambiguous resolve of a migratory warbler. In the orange and black flicker of a redstart's tail at Gumbo Limbo Park—in this altogether ordinary fall sighting—one can still glimpse a restorative vision that cuts to the essence of things.

I never saw the Cuban pewee. It never showed itself that day, and I didn't rejoin the search in the days that followed. Concerned over its fate, however, I did scan the next and final two Florida rare-bird alerts regarding the small flycatcher:

> 11/3 The CUBAN PEWEE was not seen today (11/3) at the Gumbo Limbo Nature Center on A1A in Boca Raton. Yesterday it was seen and heard north of the main building in the northwest area of the park. It was absent the day before. Its call of pit-pit-pit-pit is repeated 3 to 6 times. The bird is called Crescent-eyed Pewee in the new West Indies guide and Greater Antillean Pewee in the James Bond guide to Birds of the West Indies.

> 11/5 The CUBAN PEWEE has not been seen since 11/2 at the Gumbo Limbo Nature Center on A1A in Boca Raton.

A number of things might have happened to our little visitor from the tropics, most of them not very heartening. It may have moved on to a more remote westerly locale in south Florida, a broader swath of live oak and slash pine beyond the incessant hum of the highway; it may have been preyed upon by a skilled Merlin, sharp-shinned hawk, or peregrine falcon; it may have found fly-catching rough going in Florida and perished of hunger. I cling to a more hopeful, if fantastical, possibility. Perhaps our feathered immigrant heard a faint echo off the Atlantic, the *pit-pit-pit-pit* of a rival in the tropics. Perhaps the Cuban pewee answered the challenge. Its stomach engorged with damselfly, cankerworm, and lacewing, perhaps it gathered its bearings and flew home.

12

Geiger Tree

GEIGER TREE (*CORDIA SEBESTENA*). Native to the northern coast of South America, Yucatán, the West Indies and, possibly, Key West (its seeds float), although most experts seem to believe that the specimen was likely introduced to Florida. It's an evergreen boasting year-round clusters of orange trumpet blossoms and small pear-shaped fruit pods. The fruit is edible when raw, but fibrous. It smells better than it tastes. Cooking improves the taste, somewhat. The kernels taste like filberts. The geiger tree's fruit and kernels are reputed to treat symptoms of malaria, catarrh, edema, venereal disease, and incontinence. Its seven-inch green leaves are broad, thick, and sandpaper coarse. The geiger beetle, a flashy green bug dedicated exclusively to the geiger tree, defoliates specimens on occasion, but the trees usually recover. Geiger trees grow at a moderate rate to twenty-five feet.

I had lived in Florida for an awfully long time before I noticed our geiger trees. I was drunk on the heady new bird varieties all about in the subtropics: herons and egrets and ibises, oh my! Wendy and I traveled to the Keys primarily so that I could add yet another new species to my life-list: the threatened white-crowned pigeon. We didn't have to go very far to find the birds, only a quick stop at the Dagny Johnson Key Largo Hammock Botanical State Park at the northern tip of the Keys. The Upper Keys support the greatest tree diversity of anywhere in the United States, I was amazed to learn from my American Birding Association's *A Birder's Guide to Florida* (2005), and feature gumbo limbo, strangler fig, poisonwood, mahogany, wild tamarind, ironwood, torchwood, satinleaf, cupania, manchineel, and geiger. The two-thousand-acre park, itself, was an incredibly lush but eerily paved site of a failed residential development, planned by its would-be developers in the 1980s as an "imitation Mediterranean coastal village." Thank heavens for small mercies. As you walk, you glimpse partially buried remnants of coral walls amid the green; you reach a circular courtyard, which may have been designed as a traffic roundabout; you pass through a dank concrete tunnel beneath an abandoned roadbed. There's a vague *Planet of the Apes* feel to the place, which is instructive and precious, I think. There aren't very many places I've encountered in Florida, or elsewhere, in which you can simultaneously experience the wonder of the natural world and glimpse vestiges of what might have been had certain human designs held sway. Instead of nearly three thousand stucco homes, artificial lakes, and canals, we were treated to the sight of seven or so white-crowned pigeons cavorting high in the dense canopy of innumerable West Indian hardwoods, their wings batting loudly against the dense foliage.

"Well, that was easy," I uttered to my wife, lowering my binoculars.

I was familiar with Audubon's famous engraving of the two white-crowned pigeons, which he painted upon glimpsing the birds on his own visit to the Keys in 1832. But I had never contemplated the flora that occupies roughly half of the canvas, those audacious orange trumpet blossoms—not until I visited the salvaged acres of the Dagny Johnson Key Largo Hammock Botanical State Park, and then visited the Audubon House in Key West the next day. A guide pointed out the actual geiger tree upon which Audubon might—or might not have—observed the white-crowned pigeons. There's substantial controversy on this front. In any case, the tree now looms some thirty feet high with a trunk over fifty inches in circumference. The house, and the tree, had belonged to Captain John H. Geiger, a wrecker, hence the tree's common name. Audubon knew the tree as the rough-leaved cordia and chose it for the backdrop of his white-crowned pigeon engraving as he was terrifically impressed by the few specimens he observed. "This plant, on account of its large tubular scarlet flowers," he writes in his *Ornithological Biography, Vol. 2* (1832),

> is one of the most beautiful of the West Indian trees. I saw only two individuals at Key west, where we supposed, they had been introduced from Cuba. They were about fifteen feet high, the stem having a diameter of only five or six inches. They were in full bloom in the early part of May, and their broad deep green leaves, and splendid red blossoms, mingled with the variety of plants around me, rendered their appearance delightful.

I left the Keys invigorated by our sighting of the white-crowned pigeons and the impressive geiger tree on Key West but also somewhat chastened. Why hadn't I wondered about, or even noticed, the beautiful tree in Audubon's painting of the white-crowned pigeons? Curious, what we see and what we somehow don't. We might just as well know Audubon's painting as "Rough-Leaved Cordia" instead of "White-Crowned Pigeon," but fauna, for most of us, I imagine, tends to distract from the flora across the visual field. Even Audubon wasn't inured. If his famous engraving of the white-crowned pigeons might be said to hold a dirty little secret, it's that Audubon relied upon his assistant, George Lehman, to paint the rough-leaved cordia.

Shortly after Wendy and I arrived home, we located, purchased, and planted our own geiger tree in our front yard. And I began reading more about them. Turns out that there's quite a bit out there to peruse on the Internet. Geiger trees have become something like ground zero in the native versus exotic gardening wars in Florida. The terms of the battle are interesting, for those of us intrigued by such gardening controversies. As the tree sports such audacious orange blooms, proponents of exotic flowering trees cite the lack of definitive documentation of its existence in Florida at the time of European arrival as further proof that native Florida trees lack the showy flowers of exotics from the tropics. Meanwhile, native-plant devotees in Florida will not release their claim on this lovely specimen, and they cite ample circumstantial evidence to buttress their convictions: 1) The tree is native to Cuba. 2) Many native Florida plants of tropical origin migrated here across the Straits of Florida and the Gulf of Mexico by wind, ocean currents, and migratory birds (by way of their milky excretions). 3) Geiger-tree fruits are buoyant in seawater and viable for months. 4) That the earliest botanical accounts of the Keys failed to report geiger trees is unfortunate, but not definitive, as these accounts failed to document several native Keys specimens. 5) The existence of geiger trees on the Dry Tortugas—where John Wilkes Booth's surgeon was incarcerated—is documented as far back as 1877, and it is unlikely that the trees would have been cultivated on such a remote outpost. 6) Research suggests that the geiger beetle, which must have evolved along with its only host plant, is a native Florida subspecies. 7) John Kunkel Small and other botanists documented the fairly widespread distribution of geiger trees in the wild in the early 1900s; it is unlikely that this particular plant would so rapidly transition from cultivation in the Keys to widespread distribution in south Florida.

It would be nice to have a definitive answer to this conundrum, I suppose.

Yet even if it cannot be determined that geiger trees in Florida existed prior to Captain Geiger's trees, I'm still inclined to offer these particular specimens a native waiver. While Captain Geiger may have procured geiger-tree seeds from the West Indies in the early 1800s and planted them in his yard, as Audubon's writing and other historical accounts suggest, it seems just as likely to me that an errant Bahama mockingbird or other Cuban bird, its belly full of geiger-tree seeds, also "planted" geiger trees in the Keys, as I suspect they continue to plant them now.

In any case, Wendy and I continue to care for our geiger tree, without too much anxiety over its native bona fides. It's done pretty well over the past few years, having grown at a pace commensurate with its reputation. From time to time, it looks withered and gray on account of those pesky geiger beetles, this voracious bug that descends upon the poor tree, sporadically, devouring its leaves. But our lovely specimen, ten feet tall or so now, recovers nicely after each insult, throwing out fistfuls of orange blooms as if to spite its flashy green pest. I make it a point to look at our geiger tree, and to see the tree, wondering, all the same, what else I'm missing right in front of my eyes.

13

On Stealing Fruit

"MEXICANS STEALING YOUR LIMES." So my Italian neighbor, Franco, tipped me off about the serial theft of my Persian limes by the Latino landscapers, who maintain a separate neighbor's yard across the street.

Franco and I were out front, puttering about our respective gardens. I thanked him mildly for the information, wiping my filthy brow. I could tell by the frozen look on his face that my apparent lack of concern confused him. "I told them I call police," he continued in his dialect, "if I catch them in my yard."

I didn't think much of his warning at the time, partly because I suspected that Franco might have been wrong, and partly because my family was struggling, anyway, to keep pace with our bountiful crop of limes that season. There were only so many mojitos and limeades we could drink, only so much yellowtail snapper ceviche we could eat.

And so I'm not sure what surprised me more a few days later when I spied from my master bedroom window the two Latino landscapers stripping the fruit from my Persian lime tree (*Citrus latifolia*)—that they were, in fact, stealing my limes or that it provoked such anger in me to catch them in the act. I rushed out the front door to confront them and caught them totally unawares, each of them clutching awkward handfuls of ripe green fruit.

"What do you think you're doing!?" I accosted them. They gazed doe-eyed at me, frozen in their tracks. I wasn't sure they understood my English words, but they must have gotten the gist of things.

"You have to *ask* me if you want my limes!" I continued.

Nothing.

"Necesitan preguntame si quieren mi fruta," I took a lame stab at the Spanish.

"Here," the shorter of the two finally extended his lime fistfuls toward me. "You want? Take." His taller comrade, whose dark hair was long behind a dingy baseball cap advertising their (or, more likely, their employer's) landscaping company, extended his limes toward me, too, but remained silent. I exhaled. It suddenly felt churlish to begrudge these hardworking laborers a few measly limes when I had it so easy, comparatively—my "work" consisting mostly of gazing at a blank computer screen from within the comfort of my air-conditioned home. And, again, we had more limes than we could handle, anyway.

"No, you might as well keep them now," I uttered, my blood pressure abating. "Just, maybe, ask next time, okay?" They nodded their heads and walked back across the street with their modest harvest.

What I didn't think about at the time, but might have, was that these two landscapers were performing the rites of a longstanding ritual in my densely populated patch of Florida: the sometimes surreptitious harvest of our manifold fruiting trees about town, citrus and otherwise. To sound just a sampling of our regular bounty is to invoke the fecundity that accompanies our year-round, Zone 10 growing season: orange, lemon, lime, litchi, loquat, grapefruit, guava, papaya, pineapple, mango, avocado, tangerine, carambola (aka star fruit), sugar apple, kiwi, kumquat, banana, and so on. Most of these fruiting trees boast multiple varieties too. If you wanted to buy a mango tree from my favorite local tropical nursery, for example, you would on any given day be faced with upward of thirty varieties from which to choose.

Litchi fruit, to my mind, is the most delectable and undervalued of our local fruits. The litchi-tree (*Litchi chinensis*) variety in south Florida, the Sweet Cliff, is fairly small and nondescript for most of the year, its long leathery leaves in droopy clusters, its warty green pods camouflaged within the foliage. Given the year-round greenery and ostentatious blooms all about in Florida, I can't say I much notice these trees for most of the year, not even their modest yellowish-white flowers in the spring. But by May or June each year, the warty pods, not quite the size of ping-pong balls and somewhat oblong, announce their ripeness by turning raspberry pink. Now *this* I notice! Tiny barbs on each of their scales render the pods rough to the touch. Yet not so rough that you can't peel the skin to reveal the moist, translucent fruit inside. To plop the whole fruit into your mouth is to savor the succulent sweetness that the Chinese have appreciated for over two thousand years. Just make sure to spit out the smooth brown seed. If you've only eaten canned litchi "nuts" at Chinese restaurants, bathed in artificial syrup, you don't know what you're missing.

Many of our fruiting trees stand in private backyards, tended and harvested by homeowners, who often distribute their surplus to coworkers and friends. Luckily for my litchi-fruit cravings, I happen to know someone who knows someone who cultivates several litchi trees—an elderly female immigrant from Calcutta, who gives them away. Other homeowners are more enterprising. To take advantage of her robust mango crop this year, a friend of ours tried her hand at preparing, bottling, and selling mango salsa. Some residents erect fruit pyramids on card tables in their front yard, collection coffee cans advertising their price. Fifty cents each seems to be the going rate in my neighborhood for mango. My ten-year-old son, for his part, delivers some of our limes to one of his school friends, who operates a lemon and (now) limeade stand. They worked out some sort of percentage deal, the precise terms of which Henry hasn't disclosed.

Only an outright thief would tromp behind a fence into someone's backyard to steal fruit. But plenty of the fruiting trees in my city stand more ambiguously on the swales between sidewalk and street, land technically owned by the city, or they stand on city property, itself, around the library and city hall, or on abandoned lots, or on commercial property, where ripe fruit often languishes, unattended. There's a lot of residential transience in my area; often, homeowners who plant a certain fruiting tree for future harvest abandon their crop to new owners, who may not like oranges or lemons or avocados. Property owners often neglect their fruiting trees in plain view in their front and side yards, allowing, say, their drooping oranges to grow past ripe, some of them bursting on the sidewalk, promptly growing rancid and attracting a countless variety of vermin, including Florida rats, which like to hide by day in the dense canopy of sabal palms and do their foraging by night. In this case, you're practically doing the homeowners a favor by taking a few ripe specimens off their hands! All of which is to say that a certain gray area exists when it comes to the morality of harvesting our local fruit.

If the matter of fruit-harvesting ethics seems rather random or trivial in the grand scheme of things, I'd only point out that establishing ethical codes for this precise activity has long preoccupied humankind. In my own religious tradition, students typically begin their study of the Talmud with the second chapter of the tractate Bava Metzia, during which the rabbis over hundreds of years debated and parsed the laws pertaining to lost objects. The rabbis' arguments and counter-arguments vis-à-vis "found fruit" take up a good bit of the densely packed page space. While I won't attempt to gloss the entire chapter, the rabbis take pains to distinguish between found objects that must be announced, so that the owner can reclaim possession, and found objects that belong to the finder. Fruit in a vessel or piles of fruit, for example, must be announced. But "scattered" fruit—or scattered coins, or strings of fishes, or bundles of flax, for that matter—belong to the finder. That students tradition-ally begin their Talmud study with this chapter suggests, in part, that the rules governing our disposition toward lost objects, including fruit, form the moral bedrock on which most other laws stand. When present-day landscapers, neighbors, and I collect fruit about town, we participate, however implicitly, in this age-old dialogue governing the ethics of fruit collection.

To return to the decidedly unscattered fruit on my own property, the land-scapers from across the street really should have known better than to harvest my Persian limes without first knocking on my door to ask for my permission. True, the tree stands in my side yard, in plain view from the street, but it's not on the swale and it's clearly a well-tended tree. To my mind, they breached our local—if somewhat vague—etiquette when it comes to harvesting neighbor-hood fruit.

If the landscapers had been brazen enough to walk around to the back of my property, they would have noticed three additional specimens: a Meyer's lemon, a key lime, and a hamlin orange. My wife and I have taken to cultivat-ing various citrus trees, with varying degrees of success given the malevolent host of ever-evolving bugs and blights (e.g., canker, scale, mealybugs, mites, nematodes, fungi) that keep the USDA scientists plenty busy in their labora-tories and give commercial growers insomnia.

Cultivating citrus trees, on the face of it, runs counter to the native-plant notions that have mostly governed our landscaping choices. Indeed, it sur-prises, and disappoints, many people to learn that *none* of the prized fruiting trees in Florida are native to the state. Most citrus, for example (and even the banana and mango), hails from Asia. Yet some flora, in my view, enmesh themselves so thoroughly into the very fabric of a place that to parse their native or imported origins to establish their bona fides is to descend into ab-surdities. I wouldn't deny Italians their beloved tomatoes, even though the tomato plant, technically, is a New World fruit. In my own environs, I'm willing to grant citrus a native waiver (a courtesy I extend to the geiger tree, too), given its longstanding tenure, its noninvasive and rather short-lived tendencies, and, of course, its fruit!

It's not an overstatement to suggest that Florida, as we know it—the very layout of its towns and cities—would not exist were it not for the orange tree (*Citrus sinensis*). It seems appropriate that our standard-issue license plates feature a pair of oranges advertising white blossoms. The sweet aroma of orange blossoms lured the first pioneers to northern and central Florida in the latter years of the nineteenth century. The sprawling, fragrant orange grove at Cross Creek (near Gainesville) convinced the writer Marjorie Kinnan Rawlings to pull up stakes in frigid Rochester, New York, in 1928. Year-round living in northern and central Florida without air-conditioning and DEET was difficult in the early years. South Florida seemed an especially harsh, mosquito-infested wasteland. As Marjory Stoneman Douglas recounts in *The Everglades: River of Grass* (1947), it took the devastating winter freezes in 1894–95—which decimated Florida's citrus crop—to inspire significant settlement into the region. "The great thing then," she writes, "was to get below what they called the 'frost line.'"

Julia Tuttle, one of the first settlers to Miami, had been hectoring Henry Flagler for years to extend his railroad to her tiny outpost. Miami then consisted of only two properties: her home on the north bank of the Miami River and William Brickell's on the south bank. By the time of the freezes, Flagler had extended the railroad only as far south as Palm Beach, where he built his swanky Royal Poinciana Resort. He hadn't planned on continuing the track any farther south. Yet the harsh winter of 1894–95 changed Flagler's plans, as Michael Grunwald documents in his wonderful book, *The Swamp: The Everglades, Florida, and the Politics of Paradise* (2006). The citrus crops as far south as Palm Beach were severely damaged by below-freezing temperatures. So Flagler sent one of his agents, James Ingraham, to assess the state of affairs southward. Ingraham traveled to Miami and reported back that there had been no damage. Tuttle had met with him and, to prove that Miami sat well below the frost line, famously gave Ingraham a branch of unscathed orange blossoms to deliver to his boss. Tuttle finally got her way. Flagler bought tens of thousands of acres of land in Miami and extended the railroad, inspiring a mini-boom. Along the way, Flagler sent agents to buy up land and forge new towns. "Soon," Grunwald writes, "settlers were launching farming communities all the way down the Atlantic ridge, the so-called 'Gold Coast.' Below West Palm Beach, Michigan transplants founded Boynton Beach and Delray Beach. A Flagler engineer laid out Boca Raton; southern farmers founded Deerfield Beach and Pompano Beach."

The Flagler engineer to whom Grunwald refers, who laid out the first small portion of my town, was Thomas Moore Rickards. Flagler deployed Rickards in 1895 to buy the first tracts of Boca Raton land just east of my current neighborhood to begin, yes, an orange grove. Rickards bought fifty acres along Lake Boca Raton (a broad stretch of what we now call the intracoastal waterway), which he called the Black Cat Plantation. The railroad, Flagler knew, would prosper only if there were both people and freight to transport. Orange groves would yield oranges, fine freight for his train; the groves would also bring workers, who would need homes to live in, the materials for which would also be freighted by his train. It was tough going in south Florida, despite the railroad and increasing settlement. Rickards would move his family to the more temperate North Carolina in 1906. He and other settlers, however, would build upon Boca Raton's humble agricultural beginnings. A group of Japanese Christians, with Rickards' approval, would establish the Yamato colony in west Boca Raton, where they farmed pineapples. Other early settlers, such as Frank Chesebro, Bert Raulerson, and August Butts would also establish large farms on which they would grow mostly citrus, beans, and peppers. In 1915, Pearl City, the historic African American neighborhood in my town, was founded by Rickards and George Long, who would later become Boca Raton's first mayor, to attract a desperately needed agricultural labor force.

Addison Cairns Mizner, an architect without any formal training, forged the distinctive Mediterranean Revival look of Boca Raton, which endures today. Captivated by the prospect of designing an entire town, Mizner moved to Boca Raton in 1925 and set about developing sixteen thousand acres for commercial and residential use. The Cloister Inn and its golf course (now the Boca Raton Resort and Club) would be the centerpiece of his efforts, but Mizner also planned to build several Mediterranean Revival homes in the 1920s. Of particular interest to me here, a certain fruiting tree was a key component of Mizner's vision for the town he would practically build from scratch: the coconut palm (*Cocos nucifera*).

Palm trees, generally, and the coconut palm, specifically, played a pivotal marketing role for Mizner from the get-go. Mizner knew that he was not so much selling real estate as he was selling the prospect of a languid and carefree (if somewhat confused) tropical/Mediterranean lifestyle to prospective transplants from the Northeast and Midwest. To make his case, Mizner filled the elaborate marketing book, *Boca Raton*, which his corporation produced and distributed in 1925, with color drawings of palms and verbal allusions to palms.

Like citrus, the coconut palm is not native to Florida. Most botanists believe that the tree originates from land bordering the Indian Ocean or along the Malay Archipelago, a vast group of islands between the Indian and Pacific Oceans. But, also like the citrus tree, the exotic origins of the coconut palm seem almost beside the point, as it's long been ensconced into our local culture, given its beauty and manifold uses. Some of the most famous paintings by the Florida Highwaymen—a group of African American artists who sold their vibrantly colored Florida landscapes by the side of the road to northern tourists—happen to feature coconut palms. When I first moved here, I remember frowning upon these oil paintings, which seemed garish to my northeastern eyes. It was only after I'd lived here for a few years that I took another look at some of these paintings and decided that, yes, that's what a sunset framed by coconut palm and jacaranda and royal poinciana looks like in Florida!

The coconut palm was bound to take root in Florida, eventually. Human migrants have long transported its hardy fruit from shoreline to shoreline on their makeshift boats. Coconuts also travel far distances across the waters on their own buoyant accord to germinate on distant shores. As I'm now a fisherman, if not a very good one, I often see coconut husks bobbing into our inlet with the tide, and often mistake them for big sea-turtle heads. I always marvel at their possible origins, the Keys or the Bahamas at the farthest, I imagine, but who knows? Amazing what the tides can deliver to us, mostly when we're not looking.

The coconut palm remains an important commercial crop in many tropical countries. "If you could count the stars," an old Philippine proverb goes, "then you could count all the ways the coconut serves us." The white, fleshy layer—called the copra—grows to about one inch think just inside the shell, while roughly two cups of coconut water fills up much of the hollow inside. The sterile vitamin and mineral-rich fluid was used during World War II by both Japanese and American doctors as an IV solution for wounded soldiers. The "milk"—commonly used for cooking—is the more whitish liquid squeezed from the copra. Dried copra is pressed to extract the valuable coconut oil, primarily used for cosmetics, soaps, and margarine. In addition, sap from the flowers can be boiled down to a delectable syrup; the fruit-husk fibers (known as coir) can be woven into rope or twine; the leaves can be woven for use as roofs, fences, brooms, and brushes; dried shells can be fashioned into ladles, cups, and pots and make fine, clean-burning fuel for fires; the "heart" of the growing point at the tree's tip is the main ingredient of hearts of palm salad, even though its harvesting kills the tree. "You cannot have your palm tree and eat it too," Rawlings declares wryly in her Florida memoir, *Cross Creek* (1942).

Indeed, of all our local fruiting trees, the coconut palm may be the most useful. Yet it's also probably the least appreciated, beyond its ornamental virtues. Most residents consider the heavy coconuts a nuisance and hazard, which to some extent they are. My neighbor's untended coconut tree recently repaid him by dropping one of its heavy fruits on the windshield of his car, shattering it to pieces. Given our spate of recent hurricanes, most of us take care to have the fruits harvested by landscapers wielding climbing belts and spiked boots (which can damage the tree). Most landscapers and homeowners discard the large coconuts, leaving heavy piles on the swales for the city's weekly debris pickup. But if you pay close attention, you may witness the subtle harvest of this discarded fruit before the city's large-debris trucks with their giant claws do their weekly sweep. Residents from various Caribbean islands, or from South America—or from pretty much anywhere except the United States—can sometimes be observed picking through these piles, shaking coconuts to determine their water content, then loading the finest specimens into the trunks of their cars or beds of their small trucks. Most seem to harvest just a few for individual use, but sometimes I'll notice whole truckloads carted off, which may be the same coconuts I'll notice later sold cheap at my small local Caribbean grocery store.

A large coconut palm droops over our property from the neighbor's yard to the east (Franco, our neighbor to the west, would never tolerate a sloppy palm), and we're pretty careful about having the fruits harvested before they grow too large and threaten our tiled roof, not to mention our skulls. We give several to Willie, who scales the tree with a machete to do the harvesting, and sometimes a Trinidadian friend of ours will come by to pick up a few. He tried showing me one time on my driveway how to open the tough green husk with a machete to extract the water. While standing, he balanced the husk from its base with his left hand and, choking up on the machete with his right, dispatched a series of short, disciplined blows at a shallow angle, shaving away at the husk's crown, rotating it counterclockwise with his cradling left hand after each practiced strike. I cringed upon each blow, worried that he'd sever one of his fingers, but he must have known what he was doing. It took him only thirty seconds or so to carve open the husk, exposing the hairy shell inside. One deliberate whack at the shell and it cracked open like, well, a nut.

It's the water he and his family drink, about which he makes extravagant health claims, beyond its rich vitamins and minerals, claims ranging from kidney-stone prevention to increased virility. Coconut water doesn't taste so good to me, though. My kidneys are fine, I think, and Wendy and I don't need any additional children to feed so the virility thing isn't much of a sell! I'm not quite sure why I continue to sample this potent beverage. Maybe because the very experience of drinking from this local fruit seems somehow a meaningful activity, in the same way that it seems meaningful to eat fresh litchis and mango, to keep an eye out for the birds, to fish the Atlantic at night, and to grow my own citrus trees. To participate in our local harvest, however minimally, is to partake of something more essential and unique to my homeplace, properties that rapidly give way to the homogenizing contemporary forces of unchecked commercial and residential development. Something tells me that I ought to resist these leveling forces, that I should ever be on the lookout for ways to see my homeplace more clearly, to *be* more fully in and of Florida. Living this way offers me ballast in ways I can't claim to fully understand.

One can still glimpse a few agricultural tracts here and there in my area, but most have long ago disappeared. The nearest orange grove one town north in Delray Beach went belly up about five years ago without so much as a warning, ceding acreage to outsize stucco homes. So it goes throughout the sunshine state. The already waning commercial Persian lime orchards in Florida were decimated by Hurricane Andrew in 1992. The limes that Floridians buy in supermarkets today are all imported from Mexico. The state estimates that since 1996 Florida has lost more than 200,000 acres of citrus land, mostly to commercial and residential development. Those fruiting trees that grace our residential properties might be seen as grave markers for long defunct groves. Again, so it goes in Florida.

One would think that I'd courted some good karma through my Persian lime tree. After my initial confrontation with the Latino landscapers, I began to give them small bagfuls from time to time when I'd see them working across the street. I was feeling pretty good about things, downright smug, I admit, until I noticed the two USDA workers from my bedroom window, a man and a woman, inspecting my tree, holding leaves still attached to branches just inches away from their eyes. You can easily spot the USDA officers. They're always overdressed for the heat and laminate identity tags dangle from clips on their shirt pockets.

I rushed out to confront them. "Can I help you?" I asked, a vaguely hostile edge to my voice. I feared that they might diagnose my tree with canker, then chop it down, issuing me a paltry check to Walmart for my trouble. This was the state's policy at the time. But it wasn't canker, the short Latina USDA worker informed me after I inquired. Canker, apparently, was *so* 2002. Rather, my tree had been stricken by a psyllid, the latest scourge, also known as "citrus greening." The tiny, sap-sucking insects had been busy, apparently, introducing a deadly bacterium into citrus crops across the state. They currently represent the greatest threat to the industry. "Citrus Disease With No Cure Is Ravaging Florida's Groves," reads the front-page headline of a 2013 article in the *New York Times*. A study conducted by University of Florida scientists, the article explains, concluded that between 2006 and 2012, citrus greening cost Florida's economy $4.5 billion and eight thousand jobs.

I didn't know any of this at the time, as the USDA workers could tell, I imagine, from my blank expression. "It chokes the tree's circulatory system," the woman explained. "No cure." I suppose I still looked dumbfounded, stricken as I was, because the woman's taller, older male counterpart elaborated upon her explanation. "It's like cholesterol," he added.

For a while, my lime tree looked no worse for the wear. It continued to produce plump green fruit that we continued to enjoy ourselves and tithe to the landscapers across the street. I even entertained the notion that the USDA workers were wrong, that the tree would survive. But over several months my poor tree took a turn for the worse. Yellow now mottles most of the leaves, although I douse it often with a nutritional spray. Much of the foliage has dropped, giving the tree a skeletal look. It's not long for this world, clearly. Yet it continues to set fruit. The moxie! And so I've convinced my wife, who proposed that we remove the tree immediately after its diagnosis, that we should leave the poor thing alone for as long as possible. It seems the least we can do for this lime tree that's offered us such ample harvests.

14

Spot-Breasted Oriole

MOST LIKELY YOU'LL HEAR the spot-breasted oriole (*Icterus pectoralis*) before you see it. An impossibly clean, piercing song of two or three quarter-notes, punctuated by a final half-note rising in pitch. Sort of like a cardinal on steroids. You can hear the melody, often repeated several times, a half-block away from within your concrete block home. So pay attention.

My birding friends in the Northeast weren't terrifically impressed by my report of spot-breasted orioles in my neighborhood, as the birds aren't native to the United States. Rather, they were introduced to south Florida years ago from Mexico. As they've since "established" themselves, according to the Florida Ornithological Society Records Committee, I can officially "count" the oriole on my Florida and North American life-lists. Yet it still apparently warrants at least an unofficial asterisk beside its name. Phooey, I say.

The more seriously I immerse myself in the culture of birding (and native-plant gardening, for that matter), the more I find myself confronted by official and unofficial rules governing these activities. I don't have anything against rules, per se. If anything, I'm unusually susceptible to the manifold guidelines, laws, rules, what have you, that organize our daily lives. I don't speed while driving, nor do I pursue even semicreative exemptions on my taxes, nor do I dare exceed the recommended dosage of medications (prescribed or over-the-counter). To avoid even the appearance of impropriety, I forgo the express line at the grocery store when I get up to eight or nine items in my cart. I think I've inherited this extreme obeisance to authority from my mother, whom the rest of us in the family tease by calling her "Law and Order." There's a definite comfort in following an established set of guidelines, whether we're talking about basic etiquette or the etiquette, say, laid out in terrific detail by the American Birding Association. And so my initial reaction upon learning of the spot-breasted oriole's "introduced" rather than "native" credentials was to subdue my enthusiasm for these creatures. They didn't truly belong here. Right?

It took a while, and several sightings, for me to question the prejudice among "serious" birders against introduced species and to appreciate these birds on their own terms. One of the reasons this was possible in the case of the spot-breasted oriole was that their range in south Florida has remained limited, their population has remained fairly stable, and there's little evidence that they've inflicted much harm on native-bird competitors. The story of their introduction, then, contrasts markedly with the story of the European starling (*Sturnus vulgaris*), famously introduced to New York's Central Park in the late nineteenth century. These randy and aggressive cavity-dwellers have continued to expand their range and drive out various woodpeckers, owls, flycatchers, and bluebirds from increasingly limited nesting sites. They've made their way south, alas. We have plenty of starlings in our Florida neighborhood, great flocks of which amass on our various trees and across the electrical wires. You won't hear me utter any odes for the invasive starling. Yet it's with an almost clear ecological conscience that I can say at least a brief word for the lovely spot-breasted oriole in south Florida.

It's a gorgeous oriole. Big and heavy-billed, painted black and yellow. The heads of male birds take on a rich egg-yolk orange that oozes down the body before fading to a more yellowish-orange; black spots, sometimes just a few, sometimes more, tatter male chests and stomachs below their solid black bibs. I've had ample opportunity to observe these orioles because they appreciate the ample firebush plantings about my yard. My daughter, Sophia, often spots the pretty birds out the window and gives me the heads up. When I hear her exclaim, "Ooo . . . ooo!" from somewhere in the house, I usually know that she's spotted our orioles. We usually spot them in pairs working the foliage, dangling precariously from bowed branches while probing the small tubular flowers for nectar and nectar-loving insects with their bills.

What I love about the spot-breasted orioles is that I can't quite figure out when they'll be around. Their presence is always a novelty. Cardinals, blue jays, red-bellied woodpeckers, and doves (mourning, white-winged, Eurasian collared) are our everyday year-round birds; painted buntings are our everyday winter birds; various warblers and vireos stop by during fairly predictable weeks during their fall and spring migrations. The spot-breasted orioles loiter about the neighborhood far more frequently than the warblers and vireos, but I never know precisely when I can count on their attendance. There must be a pattern, but I haven't figured it out.

When I first started hearing their piercing song, usually while working at my desk, I'd flee the indoors to catch a treasured glimpse. "Orioles in the neighborhood!" I'd holler, halfway out the door, to Wendy and the kids. Sophia would leap to follow, more quickly than Henry and Wendy would. I have high hopes for Sophia's birding future! Lately, through self-conscious effort, I've modified my response. The special sound of spot-breasted orioles about is thrilling enough—more thrilling, somehow, without the distraction of the birds' physical appearance. And so I've taken to sitting stock-still upon hearing the orioles. I stop whatever it is I'm doing, I sit, and I just listen, usually from the computer desk in my bedroom. I'll call Sophia to my side. "Shh," I say. "Listen." The birds will typically flit about the neighborhood for a while. When they're here, they're really here. Their song grows louder as they approach—Sophia and I share a gaze, our eyes widening—and then their song fades as they visit more distant perches. Then, suddenly, we'll hear one cry right outside the window, jolting us to. I'm not sure precisely what they mean to say with their song. Sometimes—when I'm in a certain mood, I suppose—the sound of their voices seems impossibly cheerful. Other times, other moods, the sound seems plaintive. I'm not sure what Sophia hears in their song, and I can't quite bring myself to ask her. It's her song, too, to interpret as she will. Her moods, to which she's entitled, I sometimes must remind myself. It's enough to know that she, like her father, looks and listens for these special birds—established Florida residents now, like us—and savors their presence.

15

A Trip to Venus

IT WON'T TAKE LONG TO GET TO VENUS. Venus, Florida. This is what I always think when the roar of automobiles and the mad crush of people at the supermarket become too much for me and I make tracks. How short a trip it is, really, before stucco homes and strip malls give way to the saw palmetto and scrub oak of Florida's interior. A scant distance in miles and minutes that belies the real distance between places like Boca Raton and Venus. This small town, hardly a town at all, lies far beyond the line of sight of most Floridians, who don't know that places like Venus exist and would probably not visit them if they did.

I don't travel alone to Venus. It's not society altogether that I wish to escape. Truth be told, I'm a hopelessly social person. I like to share my solitude with others. In this case, my old friend Rob from my graduate-school days, who has flown down from Pennsylvania for a visit. Venus was his idea. For the slash pines and scrub oak of Venus, along with a few other "hot spots" in the Lake Okeechobee area, hold the promise of a Bachman sparrow (*Aimophila aestivalis*), a bird I have yet to glimpse.

By all accounts, the Bachman sparrow is not a breathtakingly lovely bird. It lacks the striking bill of the smooth-billed ani, a Florida specialty, and the ostentatious coloring of, say, the painted bunting. It's a fairly large, and large-tailed, sparrow, mostly gray above, though sometimes more buff, with a heavily streaked back in chestnut or dark brown. At least this is what the field guides and my companion claim. It's an elusive bird, so I'm told. Shy and secretive. It "flushes reluctantly, then drops back into the brush, where it plays hide-and-seek," Roger Tory Peterson notes in *A Field Guide to the Birds* (1934).

Rob, who has observed the Bachman sparrow on several occasions, affirms Peterson's account. Its numbers are scarce and seriously declining, according to most recent reports. "But it's not so scarce down here," Rob declares in the car while we weave between the traffic, heading north on I-95. What he means to say is that I should consider it an embarrassment that I haven't seen a Bachman sparrow yet. After living in south Florida for nearly five years, it's high time I added the chunky, dusky bird to my life-list.

Off the busy interstate, we head west on Southern Boulevard past Palm Beach International Airport toward Lake Okeechobee, at seven hundred square miles the second-largest freshwater lake in the United States. We'll have to travel around the southern edge of the lake to reach Venus to the west. Gradually, the traffic lights every half-mile or so give way to open road. The high-end German and Japanese automobiles disappear and, in their place, appear dilapidated American models and flatbed trucks. In place of the Walmarts and Home Depots behind us, countless small nurseries and fruit stands crop up suddenly beside the road. Then, these more humble business enterprises give way to an impossibly flat horizon. A large sign tells us that we have reached

LOXAHATCHEE
GATEWAY TO THE GLADES

But there doesn't seem to be much evidence of Florida's Everglades from the road. Instead, only miles and miles of sugarcane sprouts. These densely planted, droopy green sprouts, dominate the landscape. Looking deceptively fragile, these young plants will soon stretch eight feet high or so in the sky. We are in sugar country, my first encounter with the land ceded by the state, or sacrificed rather, to Big Sugar. I've brushed up on the sad history. Two devastating floods in the region killed thousands of people in the 1920s, as Zora Neale Hurston recounts in her finely wrought novel, *Their Eyes Were Watching God* (1937). In the wake of these catastrophes, the Army Corps of Engineers—in a well-intentioned but myopic effort to render the area more habitable for sugarcane and for people to harvest it—built a series of canals and levees around Lake Okeechobee and in the historic Everglades, a roughly 3,500-square-mile area of sawgrass, cypress swamp, and hardwood hammock running from the southern lip of the lake to the Florida Bay. The engineers also built the Herbert Hoover Dike along the lake's perimeter—35 feet tall and 140 miles long—and, in the 1960s, the Kissimmee River, the main tributary of the lake, was converted into the C-38, a concrete canal 300 feet wide, 30 feet deep, and 56 miles long. The transformation from natural river to constructed canal essentially drained the river's five-mile-wide floodplain. While the area remains a birding hot spot (site of the Big O Birding Festival, held annually), the channeling of the Kissimmee River in the vast region north of Lake Okeechobee has mostly supported cattle interests at the expense of wintering waterfowl.

The Everglades to the south of Lake Okeechobee have fared even worse. During periods of drought, when the water levels in the Everglades run dangerously low, the South Florida Water Management District closes the Okeechobee's floodgates to sustain the drinking water supply in Lake Okeechobee; during rainy periods, when the Everglades least need the water, torrents are released into this endangered ecosystem, flooding out countless species of nesting wading birds. Aberrant water levels aside, the rapidly deteriorating water quality continues to poison the ecosystem. Despite the sugar industry's relentless television advertisements in south Florida touting their environmentally friendly methods, fertilizer-laced water from these megafarms continues to poison the lake and, consequently, the Everglades as well. Phosphorous concentrations in the lake measure 120 parts per billion today, compared with 40 parts per billion in the early 1970s. Animal waste from the surrounding dairy and cattle farms also continues to pollute the waters. Given the combined factors of poor water quality and unnaturally fluctuating water levels, it's no surprise that according to most ornithologists only 10 percent of the historic wading bird population of the Everglades remains today and that sixty-eight plant and animal species have become threatened or endangered with extinction.

Thankfully, not all is so bleak. Spurred on by the Everglades/Florida Bay Restoration Act of 1996, the federal and state governments are in the midst of a cooperative, multi-billion-dollar effort to restore this unique and precious ecosystem. A formidable team of scientists, engineers, anthropologists, and managers representing thirteen federal agencies, six state agencies, and two tribal governments aim to return the water flow and quality to as close to its natural state as possible.

And yet . . . EVERCANE SUGAR, a modest sign advertises beside the road as we speed past. I take particular note of road signs. The language we impose upon the landscape reveals much about our vision of the land and our place in it. The word EVERCANE in small, green letters catches my eye for exactly this reason. The graceful blending of the words *Everglades* and *sugarcane* offers just the vision that we wish to see, or that someone wishes us to see—a vision of harmony between the historic, natural Everglades and our more recent, man-made agricultural endeavors. But it is a sign, I fear, that obscures true sight. For the monotonous landscape of sugarcane, sugarcane, and more sugarcane from my car window more truthfully suggests the disharmony between Everglades and sugarcane. One exists largely at the expense of the other in Florida. No point in deluding ourselves to the contrary with signs that read EVERCANE.

For a moment, in my mind's eye, instead of the green blanket of sugarcane, I see the evicted sawgrass, the great sedge that Marjory Stoneman Douglas describes so eloquently in *The Everglades: River of Grass* (1947):

> The first saw grass, exactly as it grows today, sprang up and lived in the sweet water and the pouring sunlight, and died in it, and from its own dried and decaying tissues and tough fibers bright with silica sprang up more fiercely again. . . . The edged and folded swords bristled around the delicate straight tube of pith that burst into brown flowering.

Then I see a marsh hawk rising and dipping sporadically in the air. The marsh hawk is real, not imagined. The flash of white feathers on its rump gives it away. A brown female, as opposed to a gray male. It beats its wings vigorously for short bursts, then glides effortlessly, it seems, tilting its long, outstretched wings sharply up and down as it searches the sugarcane fields below for a mouse or some other suitable prey. We pull over to the side of the road and observe.

I know I should call this bird a northern harrier, its updated, ornithologically correct, name. But "northern harrier" reveals so little about this marvelous tilting and bobbing bird of prey. So I'll continue to think of it as a marsh hawk, clinging fiercely to its southern range, struggling to make a go of it above this sugarcane field that a blink of the eye ago was its prized marshland, teeming with a delectable array of frogs, snakes, and water rats.

Back in the car, we reach the lake in a matter of minutes. Or at least the signs tell us that the lake is there. We cannot see it. I had anticipated a scenic vista across the vast, turbulent water. But the lake hides from sight behind the thirty-five-foot dike. What we do see are the towns. We pass through several of them as we trace a "u" around the southern edge of the hidden lake: Belle Glade, South Bay, Clewiston, Moore Haven—towns populated largely by the overworked and underpaid black and brown workers of the sugar industry. AMER-

ICA'S SWEETEST TOWN, a sign outside Clewiston boasts, but it doesn't seem very sweet from the road. Other signs within the town itself betray the poverty that defines the lives of these migrant and nonmigrant sugarcane workers. WIC PROGRAM, a wooden sign above a convenience store reads. FOOD STAMPS, reads another. Innumerable gas stations, fast-food restaurants, seedy liquor stores, and bars litter the sides of the road in these sugar towns. "Everglades slums," Douglas described them some fifty-odd years ago. They remain slums, but slums of the more urban, globalized variety. Asphalt highways and homogenous gas stations have supplanted the "muddy main street[s]" and "frowsy small lunchrooms" that Douglas glimpsed earlier in the century.

Suddenly, west of the lake, we find ourselves in cattle country. ENJOY BEEF, a dilapidated, yellow sign with brown letters advises. To encourage me further, the sign assures me that beef is REAL FOOD FOR REAL PEOPLE. Instead of sugarcane across the flat horizon, we see the sage-green fans of scrub palmetto, brown grasses, and dirt. Slash pines and sabal palms shoot up here and there. Dense islands of oak scrub claim patches of terrain, as well. The drowsy cattle, mostly brown and bony, seem incongruous to me amid this desert-like landscape. Cows, to my northern eyes, belong to the green rolling hills and rich-smelling soil of states such as Pennsylvania. Their nostrils breathe smoke in the crisp air. My perspective is skewed, of course. The domesticated beef cow isn't "native" to anywhere. It has been imposed upon the landscape in both Pennsylvania and Florida at the behest of our insatiable appetite for red meat.

"Hold on!" Rob commands from the passenger seat. He has spotted something perched on one of the drooping electric lines. I slam on the brakes, then head backward in reverse. Rob aims his binoculars at the bird on the wire above a thicket of oak scrub and confirms the sighting. A Florida scrub-jay. We exit the car to drink in this Florida specialty with our eyes. Its profile resembles that of a mockingbird, one of North America's most prolific residents, so I'm surprised that Rob was able to recognize the bird as we sped past it on the highway. Its distinctive markings, however, gleam in the mid-morning sun now that I have a chance to look upon it with my binoculars: the brilliant blue of its long, broad tail, its black eye-patch that contrasts sharply with its blue cap, the patches of gray on its back and belly. It shifts its tail back and forth on the wire, apparently to maintain its balance in the wind. Then, perhaps spotting a meal below, it lets out a raspy *zheep*, descends into the scrub, and disappears from view.

On account of habitat loss, many birds in south Florida have sharply declined in recent years. But scrub-jays have fared particularly poorly. Unfortunately for them, their dry habitat of low-lying oak scrub converts readily to citrus grove and strip mall. No dredging required. And hardly any individual live oaks or slash pines of an estimable stature to fret over. Why not clear the sloppy scrub for something "useful"? Scrub lacks the popular appeal of, say, Sequoia. Yet Florida's oak scrub, despite its humble appearance, is as vital, and as special, an ecosystem as California's Sequoia Forest. It just takes a bit of effort to look at oak scrub and appreciate its value, to make the connection between the scrub and the dazzling scrub-jays (and other creatures) it supports. Scrub-jays are fiercely attached to their specific range of scrub and don't take well to eviction notices. When young scrub-jays reach adulthood, rather than stake out new territory, they often assist in their parents' subsequent nesting duties, thus making the scrub-jay one of the few bird species that harbors notions of extended family. Their laudable family values, however, have not served them well. Ornithologists at the University of Florida estimate that only 3,000–4,000 scrub-jay family groups remain in existence. As long as there is oak scrub in Florida, there will be scrub-jays. If the oak scrub disappears, well, so will the Florida scrub-jay.

This either matters or doesn't matter. The scrub-jay, one might argue, fares far better in the western states, so perhaps we shouldn't lament their imminent demise in Florida. I want to stand foursquare against this view. All it takes is a bit of humility to realize that the scrub-jay stakes at least as great a claim on Florida as we do. And on purely selfish grounds, it's such a lively and lovely creature to observe. Do we really want to do without them? My existence here, I know, would be poorer for their absence.

We continue our journey at a slower highway pace. The Bachman sparrow awaits us in Venus, we hope; but, in the meantime, we'll be on the lookout for other regional specialties along the side of the road. We pass over a fairly wide stream just outside Venus and decide to stop and have a look about. Birds, like people, need water. Various egrets and herons wade in the stream and hunt. A snowy egret, in particular, catches my attention. It stands patiently on a snag that reaches above the slow-moving water. Its yellow feet contrast sharply with its black legs, which, themselves, contrast sharply with its snow-white plumage. It lunges suddenly with its sharp bill and brings up a quivering, gleaming prize that abruptly vanishes down its throat. I revel in the successful hunt. In an ecosystem that has grown dysfunctional, it gratifies me to observe things running smoothly.

Just before we enter the car to leave this rich, marshy spot (my Bachman sparrow awaits), I see a brilliant white cloud flash off into the distance, high in the northern sky. In an instant, it mysteriously disappears from view, then flashes white again. Our binoculars confirm what we suspect. An enormous flock of white ibis. There must be hundreds, no, thousands, of them in the sky! From such a great distance, we need our binoculars to see their trademark black-tipped wings, dipped in ink. All we can see with our naked eyes is the sporadic white flash of the flock as the birds turn, in concert, into the sun. It strikes me as such an unusual and fascinating sight to see in the distant sky, more dazzling without binoculars, these sporadic white flashings against the sun. You just never know what you might see when you take to the outside and look!

Then, as we lower our eyes, Rob spots a crested caracara standing on the berm of the highway about two hundred yards behind us. With giant talons, it lifts a dusty fish toward its red, fleshy face and tears into the carcass with its enormous, sharply curved beak. I should be more excited to see the crested caracara. I've seen them only once before, on a birding trip to Texas. Although common in Mexico, the crested caracara is fairly scarce in the United States, residing only in choice Texas and Florida rangeland. But, like vultures, they feed mostly on carrion, and I have difficulty warming to the species. I'm in good company. The great naturalist, Mary Austin, only begrudgingly gave the vultures their due in her landmark book of the desert, *The Land of Little Rain* (1903).

"Come on, Rob," I urge my companion, who seems quite content to observe the crested caracara through his high-powered spotting scope. "Time to dial up my Bachman sparrow."

Minutes later, we reach Venus. We are still in cattle country. The dilapidated Venus General Store boldly advertises BEER, WINE, and FEED—bovine rather than human feed, I guess. We pass several small ranches on these unpaved back roads. I see emus or ostriches grazing on one of the properties. The dusty road takes us around a sharp right turn, and Rob must brake abruptly for a large gopher tortoise ambling across to the other side. We exit the car to take a closer look. While we hover over the creature, it continues to take deliberate strides toward its destination. It's not the most exciting wildlife activity to watch, a dark tortoise that looks to be twenty pounds or so crossing the road. But we can't help marveling at this prehistoric creature hanging on to its shrinking acres of suitable sandy soil. They are champion diggers, these gopher tortoises, named such for their burrows, which stretch roughly thirty feet long and ten feet deep. Several other Florida animals, including armadillos, burrowing owls, skunks, quail, and foxes, make use of the gopher-tortoise's burrow, which is why the Florida Fish and Wildlife Conservation Commission regards the tortoise as a "keystone species." Listed as Threatened in Florida, both the tortoise and its burrow are protected under state law. Property owners must obtain a permit by the state to relocate a gopher tortoise's burrow, which does represent some measure of protection, certainly; yet tortoise numbers continue to decline along with their declining habitat. The tortoises don't always take to their new location and have been run over by cars while they amble elsewhere. For all we know, this tortoise on the road might be a "relocated" creature trying to make its way back home. "Keep fighting the good fight," my friend encourages the tortoise as it disappears into the scrub. Another splendid creature of the underappreciated scrub.

Less than a mile ahead, on the right side of the road, we reach the Venus Flatwoods Preserve, a ninety-eight-acre tract of virgin longleaf pine bought by the Nature Conservancy in 1992. A short, barbed-wire fence fiercely contradicts our usually accurate American Birding Association guide that boasts "no fee." We cannot enter the preserve. All we can do is gaze over the fence with our binoculars. I carefully inspect the low-lying palmetto scrub for the Bachman sparrow while Rob searches the innumerable tall, thin pines for a red-cockaded woodpecker. The red-cockaded woodpecker is scarcer even than the Bachman sparrow. Thanks to its tall stand of pines, the Venus Flatwoods Preserve boasts an isolated population of these white-cheeked, black-capped woodpeckers, which was one of the main reasons that the Nature Conservancy bought up the land. A quick glance across the street behind me toward the utterly flat, vacant stretch of agricultural property reveals what the probable fate of these choice ninety-eight acres would have been had the Nature Conservancy not purchased the tract. It seems a pity that the state or federal government hadn't declared this precious parcel a preserve and saved the Nature Conservancy the trouble; but as long as private ownership is the name of the game, environmental organizations like the Nature Conservancy, who thankfully know how to play this game, must remain active players.

Try as we might, we cannot spot or hear our sparrow or woodpecker. With ninety-eight acres to roam, I suppose I wouldn't loiter beside the road, either. We walk up and down the road to see what else the spot might offer. We notice the yellow flash of a pine warbler in a large shrub on the other side of the road.

Several palm warblers, their caps just taking on their rusty breeding plumage, forage on a grassy, untilled portion of farmland. We hear the melodic call of an eastern meadowlark, *see-you-see-yeeer,* but cannot spot it in the brush. On the electric wires, we spot several eastern bluebirds. Although most range maps suggest that the bluebird winters on every Florida acre, I'm not used to seeing these birds here. They certainly don't winter in my immediate suburban vicinity. I think of them as northeastern farmland birds. So it's a special treat to see them thriving in the open country of central Florida, only an hour or two from my home. The royal-blue caps and backs of the males glisten in the afternoon light. The orange rust of their chests shines brightly, as well. From time to time, they spring from their perches to pursue one of Florida's countless airborne insects.

We walk farther and reach a small parcel of oak scrub. A sharp song from somewhere amid the dense foliage commands our attention. *Drink-your-tea-ee-ee-ee.* I can't quite place the song. "A rufous-sided towhee," Rob announces. His talents far outstrip my own. The bird continues to sing loudly but remains invisible. We scan the scrub with our binoculars for several exasperating minutes. Finally, a chunky bird bobs up out of a shrub into a low branch of a gnarly live oak. Its bright colors are something to see. A lustrous black bathes its head, neck, and most of its chest. Its sides are painted with broad, orange streaks. Somehow, the colors appear too vibrant for its dusty green surroundings. But this brushy undergrowth is classic towhee territory, and one of the reasons Rob was able to identify its song so readily. The real skill is knowing what to listen and look for in any given niche. There aren't too many birds that live in the scrub and make calls similar to the rufous-sided towhee. Like the marsh hawk, the towhee's name has been updated for ornithological accuracy. The eastern and western towhees are now considered distinct species, the eastern towhee and spotted towhee. But try gazing at this bird in the Florida scrub and not thinking of it as rufous-sided!

We have one more shot at the Bachman sparrow, the Archbold Biological Station just a few miles from Venus in Lake Placid. It takes us only a few minutes to reach the station, a five-thousand-acre preserve dedicated to long-term ecological research and conservation. The station was founded in 1941 by Richard Archbold, by all accounts a rather eccentric aviator-explorer, who secured a donation from John A. Roebling to purchase the first 1,050 acres of this varied central Florida habitat. The main building, built in 1930, stretches low and long amid the taller strangler figs and live oaks that surround it. An eerie quiet makes the place seem sort of sleepy, despite the prodigious research that goes on inside. Innumerable articles and books on subjects ranging from biogeography to agro-ecology have been published based upon research conducted at Archbold. The scientists Glen Woolfenden and John Fitzpatrick, for example, studied the resident scrub-jay population for years and published an important ornithological monograph on the species in 1984.

After filling out a rather extensive sign-in form at the main building, we head toward the short nature trail open to the public. The narrow trail leads us past the few cottages that house the resident researchers and winds through a patch of Florida scrub. We are soon startled by a scrub-jay that alights on a scrubby oak just a few feet from our eyes. Its band (most of the resident jays have been banded for research purposes) is clearly visible on its leg. Black bristles at the base of its powerful bill stand out prominently. The bird appears rather tame.

The scrub grows thinner, eventually, and we reach a stand of pines, some slash pines and some sand pines. The long green needles and muscular branches of the slash pines clearly distinguish them from the more densely branched, short-needled sand pines. We spot a red-headed woodpecker clinging to the trunk of a slash pine, busily boring into the thick, scaly bark. The red-headed woodpecker is one of the more gaudily colored woodpeckers, its entire head and neck a crimson that contrasts sharply against its blue-black back, which abruptly gives way to snow-white wing patches.

True to its reputation, the Bachman sparrow proves elusive. We stand for several minutes in a choice location of palmetto scrub and listen for the sparrow's call, a tough one to discern, it seems. A variable song, Rob informs me. Usually a clear initial whistle followed by an unpredictable sequence of trills and warbles. If I hear birdsong, I decide, I'll just let him know. It's still early in the year, March, so this unshaded spot of sandy scrub is bearable for several minutes. I need only shoo away one or two biting flies. Still, it soon becomes clear that searching any longer for the Bachman sparrow will be an exercise in futility. We decide, reluctantly, to complete the short loop. In moments, we are back in the parking lot.

The parking lot, however, holds its own as a birding spot. I find that this is often the case at wildlife refuges and preserves. The variety and dispersion of parking-lot trees often proves attractive to certain varieties of birds. In an enormous strangler fig beside the old pump house, which houses a vintage 1956 fire engine purchased by Richard Archbold himself, I spot a northern parula warbler, one of my favorite warblers. A plethora of colorful features distinguish this tiny bird from its cousins: a yolk-yellow throat and chest interrupted by a chestnut breast-band in the males, two widely spaced wing bars, a green patch on the back, and the trace of an eye-ring. All of these features are clearly visible on this little male high above Richard Archbold's pump house. I strain my neck to follow its dartings through the strangler fig as it searches for tiny insects. "Birdlets," Peterson aptly described the diminutive, hyperactive warblers.

On another strangler fig we spot a yellow-bellied sapsucker. The white wing patch—not always as visible, I've discovered, as most field guides contend—stands out on this particular woodpecker and makes the identification an easy one. True to its name, the yellow-bellied sapsucker craves the sap of various trees. A fastidious little woodpecker, it bores long and straight rows of holes as it dines. The careful inspection of tree branches often reveals where the sapsucker has recently visited. We observe the bird for several moments as it scales the smooth branches of the tree. Then, it lets out a nasal call and bobs off in flight.

We spot several cardinals, a red-bellied woodpecker, and a few other warblers over the next half-hour or so. But soon it's time to go. The white light of midday has given way to the ripe orange glow of late afternoon. We leave this last birding spot of the day reluctantly. It's always difficult to return to civilization after a day of birding, but especially so when a target bird (in this case, the Bachman sparrow) still lurks somewhere unseen. A swallow-tailed kite dipping above an orchard just outside Archbold offers some solace as we drive past. Graceful flyers, these swallow-tailed kites, and dramatic in appearance: black and white plumage, deeply forked tails, and sharply angled wings.

Unlike the swallow-tailed kite, the Bachman sparrow will continue to live in my imagination alone, which is okay for now. It's not a breathtakingly lovely bird. A fairly large, and large-tailed, sparrow, mostly gray above, though sometimes more buff, with a heavily streaked back in chestnut or dark brown. It's an elusive bird, so I'm told. Shy and secretive. I have yet to lay my eyes on the creature.

16

Painted Bunting

"THEY MUST KNOW THAT THEY'RE PRETTY." So Wendy pondered the reluctance of male painted buntings to show themselves during our first few
years in Florida. We had all but spread out a welcome mat for them: pole
feeders chock full of the white millet seeds they supposedly favored, a costly
in-ground dipping pond featuring a waterfall and dripper, ample leafy cover
about to protect them from predators. Several duller green females had already
cooperated over the past couple winters by answering our invitation, but where
were their male counterparts? It seemed almost churlish of them to be so coy.

It's worth pausing here simply to reflect upon how bizarre the practice of
feeding wild animals to sustain them and attract them to our sphere would
seem to human beings in our pre-industrial age, when wild creatures needed
no such encouragement. But this is where we find ourselves, a world in which
we must daily wrestle with our complicated obligations toward the wild creatures (e.g., birds, deer, wolves) we've encroached upon, weighing these obligations against our various preferences and prejudices for and against certain
species.

Painted bunting. *Passerina ciris.* "The most gaudily colored North American
songbird," Roger Tory Peterson claims without equivocation in *A Field Guide
to the Birds* (1934). Drawings and photos of the males seem incredible. Scarlet-
red chests and rumps. Emerald-green backs. Royal-blue heads. Three bold
contrastive colors on a bird the size of a small finch—five inches long with
a wingspan of just eight inches or so. "With their vivid fusion of blue, green,
yellow, and red, male Painted Buntings seem to have flown straight out of a

child's coloring book," the Cornell Lab of Ornithology website declares. It's a bird you would expect to see in the Caribbean, South America, or Hawaii, maybe, yet they range as far north as the Carolinas and south-central United States (two distinct breeding populations). The toe-tip of south Florida, where we live, represents the painted bunting's only wintering grounds in the country. The western population winters in southern Mexico and Central America. Favored habitat includes brushlands, thickets, and woodlands, and the hedges and yards that approximate such niches. Spiders and insects and their larvae comprise the bulk of their food during the warmer months, while they rely upon seeds during fall and winter.

According to most ornithologists, painted buntings have been in steady decline since 1965, not least of all because of poaching in Mexico for the cage-bird trade. Breeding Bird Survey data from 1966 to 2000, the National Audubon Society reports, "show a significant decline of 2.7% annually for Painted Bunting across its North American breeding range." The species is identified as "an extremely high priority species" in the *Partners in Flight Bird Conservation Plan for the South Atlantic Coastal Plain*, a report spearheaded by the American Bird Conservancy in cooperation with the U.S. Fish and Wildlife Service. The plan emphasizes the importance of a stable population on the sea islands along the Georgia and South Carolina coasts and calls for 100-percent protection and restoration of the maritime woodland communities along the coastal plain, which feature shrub-scrub habitat favored by painted buntings.

In response to the bird's declining numbers, the Painted Bunting Observer Team (PBOT), a group of citizen-scientists, formed out of the University of North Carolina–Wilmington in 2005. Through observing, recording, and cataloging their sightings, members of the PBOT gather important data, including population distribution, density, and abundance, which complements the efforts of ornithologists. A trained team of the PBOT has banded thousands of painted buntings in sixty locations in the Carolinas, providing additional useful data on individual birds regarding site fidelity, dispersal and migration, life span, and survival rates. The PBOT also maintains an informative and frequently entertaining blog on its website through which the PBOT staff and interns post PBOT news and sighting reports.

It's not easy to be a painted bunting. I figured this out pretty early on in my research on the birds, still frustrated by the reluctance of the males to show themselves. Even the casual study of the data, from the PBOT and other sources, suggest the manifold challenges bearing down upon these lovely birds. In addition to human poaching, painted buntings have suffered particularly from habitat degradation and cowbird parasitism. Cowbird parasitism, specifically, is on the rise as cowbirds expand their U.S. range along the eastern seaboard, the brown-headed cowbird from the north and the shiny cowbird from the south. The specific strategy of cowbirds seems macabre, if brilliant. Female cowbirds lay their eggs in the nests of unsuspecting, smaller species. When large cowbird chicks hatch, they bully the smaller chicks of the painted buntings (and various other, smaller songbirds), outcompete the proper progeny for food, and even shove their puny rivals out of the nest, completely.

If painted buntings manage to locate suitable habitat, evade human poachers, and outwit cowbirds, their brilliant plumage surely makes them a conspicuous target for merlins and other birds of prey. Nature red in tooth and claw. Which is why my wife casually speculated that the male birds must know that they're pretty. What else accounts for their skulky ways? It's a curious conundrum, in truth. Birds don't exactly admire themselves before a mirror, so it's not as if they can know exactly what they look like. It may be that male painted buntings—merlin-lunch over millennia—have simply been hard-wired to be cautious. But I prefer to believe that Wendy is right, that male painted buntings know how pretty they are. Even though they can't admire themselves, males, notoriously aggressive, can and do look at one another, which might offer them some idea of their own visual brilliance. Birds do see in color. In fact, their complicated retinas contain four color receptors, while human retinas contain only three.

It took a few seasons, but male painted buntings finally descended upon our yard, and they did so en masse. A Technicolor infusion, suddenly, to our backyard field of view. A flock of tiny painter's palettes! Catching a glimpse of a male painted bunting at our feeder, or several of them at the same time, is now a near-daily occurrence during our winter months. Yet the sight still freezes us in our tracks, no matter how harried we might be. Peterson wasn't overselling the creatures when he described them as the most gaudily colored songbirds in North America. We've enjoyed their reliable winter presence now for the past several years, and we always mourn their departure each April, when they head back to the Carolinas to breed.

While the painted bunting's luster has yet to fade even slightly, I can't quite say the same about the rest of the bird loveliness about in the subtropics. After several years in south Florida, I found myself growing somewhat inured to the daily sight of cardinals foraging in our firebush plantings, white ibis flocks probing the earth for grubs in rhythmic unison with their curved red bills, ospreys on the wing overhead gripping their enormous mullet or bass in their talons. There's a lesson here, I think. Something about this was wrong. Wonder, of course, tends to be a reflexive, instinctive response, something that takes us by pleasant surprise, a friend sneaking up on us from behind. But it can be courted too, I think, sustained through deliberate effort. And it ought to be courted and sustained when it comes to the organic workings of the natural world. The most common—and perhaps less visually dazzling— Florida sights, I believe, are in their own way precious and wondrous. I try to keep this in mind.

While I instinctively fawn over painted buntings, I try to offer the cardinals, and ibises, and ospreys the attention they deserve, as well. I continue to set out specialized seed for the buntings, but I also stock the feeder with sunflower seeds and nuts for the cardinals and jays and woodpeckers—and for the squirrels, as well, if somewhat grudgingly. In a world increasingly hostile to painted bunting, and most other creatures, our small patch of Florida soil, and backyard patches throughout the state, is more crucial than I had dared to fathom.

17

Squirrel Matters

I SAW A SQUIRREL DIE THE OTHER DAY. It was foraging beneath one of the prouder live oaks on my university campus. I was on my way to the parking lot in the failing light of the approaching evening. Then I noticed the creature and paused on the worn grass path some thirty feet away or so to watch it do its thing. The small, scruffy squirrel was padding the ground obsessively with its front feet, as if it were preparing a pie dough. Perhaps it was burying an acorn, rather than hunting for one. Its very industry is probably what attracted my attention.

Next moment, the squirrel was dead. I saw the modified golf cart careening down the cement "walkway" toward the creature, but didn't think much of it. The squirrel was several feet off the cart's path and seemed fully absorbed in its project. But then the squirrel must have heard the approaching vehicle, because it lifted its head, then darted inexplicably toward the walkway, casting itself beneath a front tire. There wasn't time for me to shout "no!" or "stop!" or whatever other warning I might have thought to cry. There was a sound, a dull *thunk*, as if the cart had rolled over a rock rather than a squirrel's skull. My innards blanched. The driver—who hadn't the time to attempt an evasive maneuver given both his speed and the squirrel's—cried "*whoa*" and paused just past the stricken creature, which writhed now on the cement, flicking its tail erratically as if it were testing out all its parts but could only get its stupid tail to flash back and forth. I stood there, frozen, my hand over my mouth. The driver, one of our campus groundskeepers, rakes and shovels dripping out the bed of the cart, looked back at the squirrel for a moment, taking the measure of the scene, but then took off on his way. I shouted, "hey!" toward him, lamely.

I ran toward the scene of the struggle. Another squirrel, which I hadn't previously noticed, beat me to the spot and nudged its mate, or friend, or whatever, futilely with its paw, which was almost too much for me to bear. For crying out loud, I thought, was this a Disney movie!? The surviving squirrel fled a safe distance as soon as it glimpsed my presence. Some blood had spattered onto the pavement as if it were flicked from a small paintbrush, and now a tiny, dark-red pool swelled beneath the creature's skull. It was lights out for this unfortunate rodent. But it still flicked that useless tail! I should stomp its skull, I thought. Here's when a grown adult acts the part and puts the poor thing out of its misery. Yet I paused there above the doomed creature, cringing. This wasn't a bug, or a lizard, or a fish, but a mammal, and a mammal just large enough that stomping on its skull seemed utterly beyond my capacities. Thankfully, after only a few more seconds, the squirrel put me out of *my* misery, its tail slowly winding down. I stood there, frozen over the now-dead creature, brimming with life just seconds before.

Strange that the scene moved me so powerfully. I can't claim that I felt any connection with this individual squirrel. We never shared a mutual gaze, like the one Annie Dillard exchanges with a weasel, recounting this moment of transcendent contact in her splendid essay, "Living Like Weasels." But I did *see* the squirrel, both before and after its demise, which is something—more, I think, than we (or I) usually do, this actual noticing. Squirrels are so pervasive in our urban, suburban, and exurban American lives that we don't tend to notice them much. They exist somewhere beyond, or aside, our field of view. They're just there, like a nondescript shrub. Amateur naturalists of various stripes see *past* squirrels. Birders see birds; herpers see snakes, lizards, turtles, and so on; there are bug-watchers and butterfly-watchers. But fewer nature lovers take the time to observe squirrels. Even biologists who study squirrels can be awfully defensive about it. Michael Steele and John Koprowski's definitive study, *North American Tree Squirrels* (2001), opens with the chapter, "Why Squirrels?"

The prevalence of squirrel. Henry and Sophia watch the show, *SpongeBob SquarePants,* a popular cartoon about a marine sponge and his aquatic friends: lobsters, squid, sea stars, and the like. The only main character completely out of its element happens to be a buck-toothed squirrel from Texas named Sandy Cheeks, who lives in a tree-dome at the sea's floor and wears an astronaut suit whenever she ventures out. I hadn't given much thought before to this unusual member of the cartoon cast. But it makes perfect sense. Given the fecundity, determination, and grit of the squirrel—its sheer stick-to-it-ness—it seems almost plausible that a hardy specimen from Texas might figure out a way to make a go of it at the bottom of the ocean. See also: Scrat, that plucky and utterly indestructible squirrel hybrid from the *Ice Age* movie franchise. Or read Beatrix Potter's *The Tale of Squirrel Nutkin* (1903) for a fantastical story featuring Eurasian red squirrels (*Sciurus vulgaris*) who use their tails to sail across the water. The real-life squirrel in my neck of the woods, the eastern gray squirrel (*Sciurus carolinensis*), happens to be the most commonly introduced and prolific squirrel on the planet. The Invasive Species Specialist Group of the World Conservation Union includes the eastern gray squirrel on its list of "100 of the World's Worst Invasive Alien Species."

The sheer abundance of squirrel, I think, is what mostly inspires our diffidence, and even animus, toward them. If I were so inclined, I could join the Florida chapter of the Anti-Squirrel Coalition. For whatever reason, creatures we value tend to be the most scarce or those unique to a particular region or habitat. In Florida, we think of alligators, crocodiles, manatees, panthers, roseate spoonbills, pelicans, egrets, and herons. We don't think much of squirrels, even though (or, rather, because) they're all about, scampering well within our field of view. All the same, I want to contemplate squirrels for a time, this most common and familiar Florida animal, every bit as dear in its own way, maybe, as Florida specialty creatures.

I shouldn't overstate our collective diffidence toward squirrels, for there have long been unabashed squirrel-lovers among us too. Roughly one hundred and fifty years before Steele and Koprowski's contribution, Thoreau studied squirrels up-close. In "The Dispersion of Seeds," a book-length manuscript unpublished at the time of the writer's death, the transcendentalist dedicates several pages to squirrel observation and reflection. He followed squirrels around the Concord woods for hours, watching them forage for pinecones and acorns and documenting the distance they traveled from host pines and oaks with the fruits of their labor, where they buried the nuts, and what trees sprang up next season in the wake of their efforts. He was particularly awestruck by the critters' industrious and ingenious labor vis-à-vis the pesky pinecone. John Muir, for his part, was enamored by the feisty Douglas squirrels (*Sciurus douglasii*) he encountered in the California backcountry. Like Thoreau, Muir was perplexed by the impossible cleanliness of these pine-cone eaters. "Strange to say," he writes in his most popular book, *My First Summer in the Sierra* (1911), "he never seems to get himself smeared with gum, not even his paws or whiskers—and how cleanly and beautiful in color the cone-litter kitchen-middens he makes."

Squirrels store and eat the fruit of pines and oaks. Pretty much everyone knew this during Thoreau's day, and Muir's day, and most everyone (though I sometimes wonder) knows this today. The precise method with which squirrels strip the cones and open acorn shells either matters or doesn't matter. I believe that it matters, and the more I learn about squirrels, the more it seems that the creatures matter, generally.

Squirrels, one might argue, won the Revolutionary War for the United States. This may be a bit of an overstatement, but it's true that the Pennsylvania rifle, crucial to the efforts of American Revolutionary soldiers, was designed specifically for squirrel hunting. Which is something. Squirrel hunting permeates William Faulkner's "The Bear," although the endeavor doesn't come off so well in this famous story. The prevalence of squirrels as quarry, instead of bears and bucks, signals the devastation of Faulkner's Big Woods by farming and timber interests. The railroad having been laid, the farms and timber companies having cleared much of the Big Woods, the bucks and bear having been all but extirpated, all that's left, Faulkner suggests, are these small squirrels.

Squirrel hunting, despite Faulkner's somewhat jaundiced view, has long been an integral part of Americana, and remains so. In 2006, 1.8 million people hunted squirrels in the United States, according to the *2006 National Survey of Fishing, Hunting, and Wildlife-Associated Recreation*, conducted by the U.S. Fish and Wildlife Association. Only rabbit and hare proved slightly more popular as small-game quarry that year, attracting 1.9 million hunters. The decidedly more prestigious quail, incidentally, attracted only 1 million hunters. "We would hunt squirrels and rabbits and coons, and whatever," one of the early, black residents of my town remembers in Arthur S. Evans Jr. and David Lee's *Pearl City, Florida* (1990). Although not too popular anymore in my densely populated area, hunting is all the rage in the scruffier outposts of Florida. And plenty of Floridians continue to hunt squirrel, specifically. There were 96,000 small-game hunters in Florida in 2006. Florida's squirrel hunting season, limited to the prolific eastern gray, extends from November 14 to March 7. The three Florida subspecies of the diminishing fox squirrel (*Sciurus niger*) are protected from hunting, thankfully. The fox squirrel spends more time foraging on the ground than the smaller eastern gray squirrel does and prefers bigger pine flatwoods and mixed pine hardwood and cypress stands with open understories, habitats on the decline owing to ranching, agricultural, and residential development interests. Increasing fire suppression in populated areas has also harmed the fox squirrels, as naturally occurring fire keeps the understory clear and favors the longleaf pines critical to fox-squirrel nesting. While fox squirrels of the western panhandle seem to be doing okay, the Florida Fish and Wildlife Conservation Commission classifies the Sherman's fox squirrel of central and northeastern Florida as a species of special concern and classifies the big cypress fox squirrel of the Everglades as threatened.

Where there's hunting, there's food. "We are all in complete agreement on squirrel meat," Marjorie Kinnan Rawlings writes in her Florida memoir, *Cross Creek* (1942). "Fried, smother-fried with a rich gravy, or made into a pilau, we esteem it highly." Early editions of the classic, *The Joy of Cooking*, include various recipes for squirrel entrees. While squirrel meat may no longer be au courant (for one thing, it's unusually high in cholesterol), there are still plenty of squirrel-eaters out there. My quick Internet search for "squirrel recipes" resulted in 192,000 hits. I'm as adventurous as the next person, but I can't claim any desire to sample squirrel meat. For one thing, I'm already battling an unfavorable HDL/LDL ratio. I'd only like to learn something more about these creatures so that I can offer them the respect they deserve, and so I begin with Richard W. Thorington Jr. and Katie Ferrell's eminently readable *Squirrels: The Animal Answer Guide* (2006). Squirrels, I discover, belong to the order Rodentia (which also hasn't helped their PR among humans) and the family Sciurdae and from there can be divided into five subfamilies. Their common ancestor lived some thirty to forty million years ago. Across five continents are scattered 278 individual species. Eight species of tree squirrels (e.g., the eastern gray) can be found in North America, along with two species of flying squirrels and fifty-six species of ground squirrels. FYI: groundhogs, chipmunks, and prairie dogs . . . all squirrels! Their diverse ranges include deserts and the wettest rain forests. Yet Australia and Madagascar are bereft of squirrels.

While tree squirrels are not considered to be "social" animals, eastern grays sometimes nest communally during the winter. A frenzied mating chase precedes copulation between the estrous female and one or more males, who must compete against each other, and the capricious female, for access. Gestation lasts between thirty-nine and forty-four days before the mother gives birth in her nest of leaves, bark, and/or grass. North American tree squirrels typically give birth to a litter of two to four babies and nurse their altricial young for sixty days or so.

These young grow into highly specialized bodies. I'll spare you most of the details, but the squirrel's most interesting anatomical feature may be the mobility of its joint between the most proximal ankle bone and the heel bone, which enables the squirrel to turn its hind feet 180 degrees around from the forward orientation so that it might pause and hang when coming headfirst down a tree. This dexterousness, no doubt, helps squirrels avoid injury. Curiously, some squirrel species don't have this joint mobility but still manage to turn their feet around while heading down a tree. No one knows, precisely, how they do it! You've probably noticed a squirrel hanging upside down like so from its feet, pausing to take your measure or to gnaw on an acorn.

Which brings me to the topic of squirrels and food, and squirrels and me. It's not quite accurate to suggest, as I suppose I have, that I hadn't actively contemplated squirrels before I saw one killed by that modified golf cart on my university campus. Because, come to think of it, I had actually watched squirrels quite a bit prior to that afternoon. More, I felt a certain way about squirrels. In short, they drove me mad and I hated them, as a teeming horde of the rodents frustrated my efforts as a bird-watcher. They monopolized my bird feeder for hours at home while the birds watched futilely from nearby perches, and while we watched futilely from our own perch at our kitchen bar. To complicate matters, and as I detailed in chapter 7, our neighbors next door began to complain about our bird feeder, which they felt had lured the squirrels to the general vicinity of their tomato garden.

We tried everything, including many of the strategies proposed by Bill Adler Jr. in *Outwitting Squirrels* (1988). But nothing worked until my son, as I've mentioned, alerted me to the device called Twirl-a-Squirrel. "The thing is, they've got nothing else to do," one of my friends observed while we were still struggling. It was an offhand joke, but he was onto something. After all, the squirrels' raison d'etre was the obtainment and ingestion of enough calories to remain alive so that they could be swift and strong and secure a mate and reproduce with gusto, or nurture newborns with their milk, and thereby sprinkle their genes about. Clearly, it was worth it to them to devote all the intellectual energy it might take to raid my bird feeder, while, as a fairly typical adult in our American society, I was beset with additional obligations.

This whole business of the squirrel's diet, I now know, is far more complex than I ever fathomed when I was mostly busy trying to *keep* them from eating. Trees and squirrels, for one thing, have co-evolved in curious, even fascinating, ways. Squirrels and their pines and oaks have over millennia enjoyed an antagonistic codependency that I tend to associate with longstanding human marriages. Oak trees need creatures to distribute their acorns; yet it's not in the oak's genetic interest to make it too easy on nut-eaters that won't bury and lose (i.e., plant) several. And so oak acorns contain tannin, a defensive chemical that makes them unpalatable and indigestible to many mammals. Further, acorn shells are designed toward an optimal level of opening difficulty. If the acorn's meat were too easy to procure (like the seeds in my feeder), then various predators undeterred by the tannins would gain too easy access and deplete the crop. Alternatively, if the acorn shells were too difficult to pry open, if the energy the task demanded outstripped the caloric payoff, then squirrels wouldn't bother to gather and scatter-hoard them in the first place. Fortunately for the eastern gray squirrel, and the oaks, these creatures who mob my bird feeder beneath the canopy of some fine live oaks can digest acorns with unusually high levels of tannin, while their teeth, jaws, mobility, and vision are well suited for acorn procurement, handling, and chewing. It's no overstatement to suggest that we wouldn't have oak trees without squirrels, and that we wouldn't have squirrels without oak trees. At least not the creatures we know as squirrel, the trees we know as oak. "A fauna and flora," Aldo Leopold writes in his classic, *A Sand County Almanac: And Sketches Here and There* (1949), "by this very process of perpetual battle within and among species, achieve collective immortality."

I decide that I'll watch squirrels for a time. Really watch them. I know that I don't have the time or the training to contribute any new knowledge on these creatures. Rather, it's the very act of watching that might put me in a new place, a more vital present, the place where any number of our finest nature writers linger, whether it be Annie Dillard watching praying mantises in *Pilgrim at Tinker Creek* (1974), Barry Lopez watching tundra birds in *Arctic Dreams* (1986), Rachel Carson watching black skimmers in *Under the Sea-Wind* (1941), or Peter Matthiessen watching blue sheep and the Himalayan mountains, themselves, in *The Snow Leopard* (1978).

I live in suburbia, so I'll watch squirrels.

The first thing I notice, scanning live oaks for squirrels at a local park, is how many big leafy squirrel nests darken the canopies. I'd never noticed them before. How often, after all, do we look up? I spot and observe squirrels in and around these trees over the next several days, and I also watch the squirrels loitering on and around my bird feeder at home. I watch them foraging in the mulched earth, making rapid cleaning swipes at their faces with their tiny hands, scratching their ears with staccato feet (fleas?), twisting their heads all the way around to gnaw at their rumps (more fleas?), chasing each other madly here and there (mating?), twitching their tails upon their chirpy vocalizations. I take note of each discrete behavior I see and speculate upon its function. Truthfully, however, I'm not so good at this looking-business. After mere minutes of watching each day, my mind begins to wander onto family matters, or e-mails I need to send, or phone calls I need to make, or student papers I need to read. I can't shake the nagging feeling that more pressing matters await my attention.

I try harder. I clear my head. There's really nowhere else I need to be, and nothing else I need to do. I get better at watching squirrels, though I never get particularly good at it, I must confess. I extend the duration of my daily observations to an hour at a time, then longer. I'm particularly taken with the squirrels' manual dexterity when handling food items, the way they rotate sunflower seeds between their tiny paws and their front teeth, the way they pat the ground, methodically, one hand after the other, when burying certain food items. Eating and burying. Eating and burying. It takes up, it seems to me, an inordinate amount of their time.

Out of the field and back to the books. Squirrels, I learn, don't simply bury and eat acorns. One need only dip into the research on the eating versus caching phenomenon to gain a definite respect for the squirrel. It's been known for quite some time, for example, that squirrels frequently excise the embryo of white oak acorns before burying them, preventing the germination that reduces their nutrition content. They've even been observed digging up acorns they've already buried, excising the embryo, then reburying the fruit—an activity that approximates, I suppose, our transfer to the freezer of perishable food in the refrigerator that we thought we'd eat earlier. Scientists have also determined that eastern gray squirrels tend to eat the acorns of white oak trees immediately, while they prefer caching the acorns of red oak trees. They've entertained any number of explanations for this behavior, weighing the differences between red and white oaks.

Red oak acorns, as Steele and Koprowski explain, have a higher fat content than do white oak acorns, and higher tannin levels too. They also germinate much later than white oak acorns. Building upon the earlier research of Peter Smallwood, John Fox, and others, Steele and Koprowski conducted an ingenious set of experiments to determine whether the contrasting tannin content, germination schedules, and/or size and handling issues vis-à-vis red oak and white oak acorns influenced the squirrels' eating versus caching strategies. What they discovered through painstaking experiments and counter-experiments was that the later germination schedule of red oak acorns accounted for the squirrels' preference to bury red oak acorns and eat white oak acorns. Moreover, the squirrels proved extraordinarily savvy about all this. Through finagling rather mercilessly with red- and white-oak acorn shells and their contents, Steele and Koprowski determined that squirrels "can detect whether acorns are dormant, and they respond by consistently caching the dormant seeds." Given their several failed attempts to confuse the creatures, they admit that they don't quite know how the squirrels recognize the dormant seeds.

And so, yes, as my friend joked about my bird feeder woes, the squirrels have nothing else to do, but what a thing it is that they do!

We don't tend to credit animals their possible thoughts on, or planning for, the future. It seems a decidedly human realm of activity—retirement plans, college funds, wills, and the like. Most of us assume that blind instinct alone motivates them. But who's to say that squirrels don't know what they're doing? Leading scientists certainly credit the squirrel with long-range planning. Strange (and wrong) that it's not seen as a particularly admirable quality to "squirrel away" our possessions.

None of this makes me feel any better about the violent demise of that eastern gray squirrel on my university campus. It might have been up to any number of complex activities, I now know, moments before it darted beneath the wheels of that careening, motorized cart. It happened to have been foraging beneath a live oak, a member of the white oak subgenus. But there are plenty of laurel oaks on campus, as well, members of the red oak subgenus. So the squirrel might have been burying or reburying a laurel oak acorn beneath the live oak tree, or it might have been digging up a live oak acorn to excise its embryo and prevent its rapid germination, or it might have been sifting the grass for live oak acorns, which it would immediately consume. It was absorbed in the busy activity of being a squirrel, which I realized at the time, and which bothered me enough after its squirrel-being was abruptly snuffed out. But being a squirrel, I now know, means enacting a series of complicated inferences and actions with an eye toward the future, a future that has nothing to do with our strange motorized vehicles. Even the critter's misguided mode of evasion suggests the utter disconnect between squirrels and us. Over millennia, squirrels have developed an erratic, "squirrely" strategy for eluding four-legged predators; it hardly seems their fault that the sudden emergence of our four-wheeled menaces renders such maneuvers obsolete. All of which bothers me even more. I'm prepared to ascribe a good bit of thoughtfulness to these creatures now.

Contemplating squirrels prompted me to take a look back at a Gerald Stern poem I've long admired. The poem's speaker comes across a scene of roadside carnage, not unlike the scene I observed on my university campus, and resolves to be "unappeased at the opossum's death." Rather than shrug off the commonplace country sight, Stern's hero touches the dead creature's face, stares into his eyes, and pulls the poor opossum off the road. It took me a fair bit of scientific research to approach, even, the empathy Stern's hero poignantly enacts. At the time of the incident, I didn't dare touch the dead squirrel but called campus grounds to come clean up its mess. Yet I wonder now whether Stern's hero knows only what we all instinctively know about most nonhuman animals but choose to unlearn—that they're persons, in a very real sense, albeit nonhuman persons. It's only more convenient to think otherwise, to be highly selective in our mercies, which we might consider distributing more widely.

18

Thoreau in Florida

A WORD TO THE WISE: leading your Literature and the Environment class on a field trip to the Everglades in the middle of August is, generally speaking, not such a great idea. But what was I to do? I had been assigned to teach the course during the summer session, and I had resolved early on in my academic career to be the "cool" professor—the sort of professor who would naturally wake up before dawn to lead a short bird-watching expedition in order to render the reading assignments more palpable and meaningful to my students.

So here we were on a Sunday morning at the Arthur R. Marshall Loxahatchee National Wildlife Refuge, the last surviving remnant of the Northern Everglades. As soon as I exited my car and felt Florida's moist summer breath on my face, then the sting of a mosquito on the back of my neck, I realized that my students' semester probably wouldn't be culminating in the rich, transcendental experience that I had planned for them.

Truth was, Thoreau's *Walden* hadn't gone over with the class as well as I had anticipated. They seemed to prefer, well, just about all the other writers on the syllabus. I had selected readings from a multicultural cadre of authors who addressed various, often contrastive, environments. For example, we explored the Nebraska prairies and farmland through the eyes of Willa Cather's Swedish immigrants, but also examined what the California grape orchards meant to Helena Maria Viramontes's migrant farmworkers in *Under the Feet of Jesus* (1996) and what a Mississippi swimming hole meant to the son of a sharecropper in Richard Wright's *Uncle Tom's Children* (1940); we explored Aldo Leopold's Sand County in Wisconsin, but also explored the urban environments rendered so poignantly in Junot Diaz's stories and Alfred Kazin's memoir, *A Walker in the City* (1951). For all my noble efforts to adopt an eclectic, broad-minded approach to our subject, however, I never relinquished my hope that Thoreau's transcendental vision would resonate most powerfully with the class, that he would somehow define our collective sensibility.

Yet it hadn't worked out that way. They found him remote, in every sense, holed away all by himself, domesticity be damned, in his tiny cabin in the Concord woods. While I hardly wanted them to light out to the nearest cypress swamp and take up a solitary existence, I had hoped that Thoreau's exhortation to his nineteenth-century readers, "Simplicity, simplicity, simplicity! . . . let your affairs be two or three, and not a hundred or a thousand," would compel them to examine whether their own frenzied lives were being "frittered away by detail"—whether, say, it was necessary or desirable to bring their various smart-devices to class. Further, I had hoped that Thoreau's excursions and revelations would inspire them to seek out their own experiences in Florida's nature, their own revelations. I had wanted them to love Thoreau, but instead they found him (and, increasingly, me) strange.

After the first few dispiriting class sessions on *Walden*, I figured that the very strangeness of Thoreau's New England to my Floridian students accounted for the disconnect. Thoreau, indeed, never visited Florida, nor did he have much to say about the American south, generally. An avid reader of travel literature, he did read Theodore Irving's account of De Soto's *Conquest of Florida* (1851) and William Bartram's *Travels* (1791). There are a few abstruse references to Florida in his *Journal*, as well. That said, the region largely failed to excite his imagination. When he sought out wilderness, symbolically, he tended to look toward the West and seemed to make his peace with his alienation from the South. "[T]hough we may be estranged from the South, we sympathize with the West," he exclaims in his essay "Walking." In a life tragically cut short by tuberculosis, he made very few actual excursions beyond his native Concord. But when he did seek out wilderness, literally, he tended to travel north, to the Maine woods and to Canada. His 1854 trip to Philadelphia would represent his most serious flirtation with the equator. So, was it simply that the flora and fauna of Thoreau's *Walden,* however brilliantly rendered, remained intangible to many of my students?

This certainly appeared to be the case. "I don't understand, isn't a chickadee just a baby chicken?" one of my students, a native Floridian, inquired after we read the famous "Sounds" chapter. I had anticipated having at least one or two such hopeless urbanites in the class, so I wasn't exactly surprised by the question. What I did find troubling, however, was that nearly all of her peers, rather than chuckle to themselves, looked expectantly toward me to answer the question. To make the strange a bit more familiar, I played a recording during the next class session of many of the northern songbirds Thoreau describes in *Walden,* most of which my students had neither seen nor heard. I think most of them appreciated the gesture. Yet, somehow, my professorial ethos suffered an irrevocable blow after this class. "You don't . . . like . . . *own* that CD, do you?" a student asked as I packed up my boom box, obviously concerned for her professor's sanity.

The situation, I gathered, was graver than I had imagined. For it wasn't merely that Thoreau's nature struck them as alien. Something about growing up and living in south Florida had cultivated (pun intended) an aversion to nature, generally. This surprised me, given the proximity of the ocean and the Everglades; yet it probably shouldn't have, given the texture of the immediate landscape, and the texture of most of my students' lives. My university catalog describes the area as a "suburban residential community," but the phrase hardly does justice to the urban sprawl that defines south Florida's constructed landscape: the bumper-to-bumper traffic on its six-lane surface streets, the seemingly infinite array of strip malls sandwiched between gated developments of identical stucco homes standing shoulder to shoulder on zero-lot plots, the incessant roar of the semis on I-95 and of the Florida East Coast trains. As our campus grows, the native burrowing owls and gopher tortoises find themselves squeezed into smaller and smaller swatches of habitat. Our new behemoth football stadium has supplanted much of our remaining acreage of oak scrubland.

The unconstructed, natural realm may be just minutes away from where most of my students live, but it remains as remote to them as Zanzibar (or the Everglades) was to Thoreau. Our modest excursion through Loxahatchee, I hoped, would restore their local environment to them. They would never observe a chickadee in south Florida or the thaw of lake ice that so inspired Thoreau's imagination, but perhaps they would find a blade of sawgrass an interesting subject for contemplation, as well. This was what I had hoped, but I couldn't help but detect a discernible lack of enthusiasm as we ambled along the Marsh Trail, an unshaded latticework of grass and dirt trails that border impoundments where the water levels are managed to support a wide array of wading birds and to discourage non-native plant growth. This being summer, the trail wasn't exactly teeming with bird life. While there were a few resident species to observe—a great egret, a great blue heron, a green heron, some moorhens and coots—there was a discernible absence of birdsong in the air. Most of the songbirds were miles away in their breeding range around Thoreau's Concord and farther north in Canada, and as the morning stretched on they seemed all the smarter for it. It was hot, and growing hotter by the minute as the unrelenting subtropical sun stretched into the sky above the row of wax myrtle and cypress bordering the refuge to the east. By eight o'clock in the morning, my T-shirt was already soaked through with sweat. We had all lathered ourselves in DEET, so a slightly nauseating chemical cloud accompanied us, which didn't seem to deter the clouds of gnats from blocking our vision. Sharp burs from untended stretches of the trail dug beneath our socks around our ankles as we dodged fire-ant holes and sluggish lubber grasshoppers that we, nonetheless, heard crackle beneath our feet from time to time.

I was leading them westward toward a vista of the Everglades, but the trek was turning out to be longer and more arduous than I had expected. So long and arduous that I couldn't help but contemplate the legal ramifications should one of my students suffer from heat exhaustion and lodge an official complaint against me. Should I have had them fill out waivers? Were my union dues all paid up? We decided to press on and eventually reached the vista. My students, however, panting from exertion, seemed rather unimpressed with the flat expanse of green and brown sawgrass before them. "This isn't very Thoreauvian," one of them complained, half-jokingly. How alien, indeed, did the most ebullient sections of *Walden* seem now even to me.

I experienced something of an epiphany just then, longing for the protective shade of the Concord woods. It wasn't simply that the local environment alienated my students from Thoreau. Thoreau, at least to a certain extent, had alienated *them* from their local environment. Or, at least the Thoreau I chose to present to them, which is the same Thoreau that lives in the popular imagination—the optimistic, transcendental Thoreau embodied by *Walden* and by the select quotations that various entrepreneurs choose to emblazon on T-shirts and coffee mugs.

Yet the Thoreau who emerges most forcefully in *Walden* wasn't the only Thoreau, just the only Thoreau I chose to present to my class. Much of the material in his voluminous *Journal* (which he never intended for publication) and several of his essays (which he did) reveal a side of Thoreau not at all certain about the "indescribable innocence and beneficence of Nature." An unmistakably "grim mode," as Joyce Carol Oates put it, pervaded Thoreau's ruminations concerning nonhuman nature. Thoreau's "Ktaadn," which documents his 1846 ascent of Maine's highest mountain, most richly evokes this mode. Thoreau was living at Walden Pond at the time, and this first foray into the Maine woods (he would return in 1853 and 1857) presented a formidable challenge to the optimism he so wished to affirm in the masterwork that he had just begun to write.

Unlike the Concord woods—increasingly domesticated during Thoreau's day by farms and cabins, and tamed by ice harvesters, loggers, and railroad workers—the Maine woods appear impervious to humankind. And, curiously, rather than inspire Thoreau, this sends him reeling. Immersed in a realm more grim and wild than he had anticipated—as grim and wild as the Everglades on a summer day—Thoreau suffers something of an existential crisis: "What is this Titan that has possession of me?" he cries. "Talk of mysteries!—think of our life in nature,—daily to be shown matter, to come in contact with it,—rocks, trees, wind on our cheeks! the *solid* earth! the *actual* world! the *common sense! Contact! Contact! Who* are we? *where* are we?"

Why hadn't I included "Ktaadn" on my syllabus? I was certainly aware of the essay. It occurred to me that I had meant, if only subconsciously, to protect them from Thoreau's dark side. I had wanted them to exult in Thoreau's optimism, not wallow in his cynicism and self-doubt. Yet this was precisely the wrong way to go about things, for a whole host of reasons, but not least of all because I had winded up reaffirming the popular, distorted view of Thoreau, and had thereby reinforced their distorted view of nature, itself. Nature to them, I realized standing beside my students at the edge of the Everglades, meant the deciduous forests, babbling brooks, and quaint ponds of Thoreau's Concord, not the impossibly flat blanket of sawgrass that stretched out before us at Loxahatchee just west of the impoundments; nature meant the melodic trill of the wood thrush, not the cacophonous clacking of a wood stork's bill. Small wonder that to many south Floridians, our wet and dry prairies, our dwindling acreage of scrub oak and palmetto, seem to be "empty" spaces, perfect for a strip mall, or a football stadium. How thoroughly—and frighteningly—the canonization of a single work had informed our perceptions of the "American" landscape. How thoroughly, in the bargain, had it cannibalized its author, whose complexity, thoughtfulness, and, finally, humanity only fully emerges upon reading *beyond* his masterwork—upon reading a Thoreau who tries and fails, often poignantly, to synthesize his Transcendental precepts with his actual experience in the natural world.

Back at the Loxahatchee Visitor Center parking lot, discouraged by the way the morning had turned out, I suggested that we take a quick spin around the boardwalk of the cypress swamp nearby. Just a remnant of the swamp that once stood here, these few remaining acres invariably depress me, so I usually avoid the boardwalk altogether. Rarely have I glimpsed the wildlife just barely supported by the dwindling ecosystem: river otters, red-bellied and pileated woodpeckers, prothonotary warblers, screech owls, yellow-billed cuckoos. I had certainly never glimpsed a songbird so late on a summer morning. So I was struck fairly speechless upon hearing a clean, unmistakable song echo through the swamp just as we stepped foot onto the boardwalk. *Tea-kettle, tea-kettle, tea-kettle, tea!* I halted in my tracks as the bird flitted onto the trunk of a nearby cypress festooned with bromeliads and Spanish moss, its white eyebrow stripe in clear view to all my students. "It's a Ca- . . . Ca- . . . Ca- . . ." I stammered excitedly, embarrassingly, " . . . a Carolina wren," I finally summoned the words past my lips. The spritely bird might have flown right out of the pages of Thoreau's *Walden.* It remained visible for a long minute or so, flitting from branch to branch before finally disappearing into the swamp.

"Wow, that's a bird that Thoreau would have seen, huh?" one of my students inquired, still gazing after the wren through his binoculars. Yes, but it was their bird too, I emphasized. A year-round Florida resident. Through seeing and hearing this Carolina wren, the same bird Thoreau had seen and heard, my students had finally established a relationship of sorts with this author, who had seemed so remote to them before. I didn't share this thought with the class, who found me odd enough as it was. In any case, it wasn't necessary. A small bird had offered a few students the valuable gift of a glimpse. They had made their Contact.

19

Ivory-Billed Woodpecker

THE IVORY-BILLED WOODPECKER (*Campephilus principalis*) principally ate grubs and grubs alone, as its scientific name suggests. This partly explains why it fared so poorly compared to its less finicky cousin, the pileated woodpecker. But at one time, and for a long time—before mass Euro-American settlement, deforestation, suburbanization, swamp dredging, cattle grazing, and so on— the limited range of the ivory-billed woodpecker included the entire soggy Florida peninsula. My home state, after all, once boasted acres upon acres of old-growth bottomland swamp forests and a stable (if never particularly abundant) population of these majestic woodpeckers. It's a miraculous thing to consider from the current vantage, ivory-billed woodpeckers throughout Florida, from Tallahassee to the Everglades. "Lord God," those lucky few ex- claimed upon catching a glimpse of the ivory-billed woodpecker, which ex- plains the bird's nickname, the Lord God Bird. What must this woodpecker have looked like to have earned such a nickname? I have an idea, of course, as we still have drawings, photographs, some black-and-white reel footage, and museum specimens. But what must it have looked like vital and alive, tear- ing through the decaying bark of a tupelo or cypress tree with its formidable bone-white bill, its nasal *kent*-calls and clearer tooting notes echoing through the swamp!?

The world grew a bit larger for a while there in 2005, after the announce- ment of several confirmed sightings in 2004 of an ivory-billed woodpecker in the Big Woods of Arkansas. The last confirmed sighting of the bird prior to that was in 1944. Pretty much every recent North American bird-watching guidebook has written off the ivory-billed as "extinct" in its prefatory pages, alongside an increasing handful of unlucky cohorts, like the passenger pigeon and Carolina parakeet. For birders like me, who still swear by Roger Tory Peterson's 1934 *A Field Guide to the Birds*, there has always been something poignant about flipping through the book and chancing upon his drawings of the ivory-billed smack in the middle of the guide alongside the other wood-peckers, the caption reading, "near extinction." Peterson didn't know it yet, but they would all be gone soon. Or perhaps not! Could Peterson's dated entry on this grandest of North American woodpeckers have been accurate, after all? "This rarest of North American birds," Peterson writes, "may be known from the Pileated Woodpecker by its larger size, ivory-white bill, large white wing patches *visible at rest,* and different underwing pattern." There's something brave and hopeful about Peterson's active, present-tense voice as he describes the ivory-billed woodpecker.

When the news of the confirmed sightings broke in 2005, I wanted to go find this bird and add it to my life-list, but something gave me pause. Most people on my college campus, with whom I breathlessly shared the news, asked me whether I had already packed my bags, which to my mind raised larger ques-tions: to what extent should the most imperiled wilderness be sought out and made accessible? How do we ascribe value to wild places and animals we may not ever see in our lifetimes? These are questions at the center of our current national debate over the management of our national parks and refuges (e.g., fishing regulations in the Everglades, the prospect of oil-drilling in Alaska's Arctic National Wildlife Refuge, the extent of the terrain on which snow-mobiles should be allowed to roar through Yellowstone). I, myself, subscribe to Aldo Leopold's call for human restraint and humility in his landmark work, *A Sand County Almanac* (1949). He decries our human tendency to value only that which we can see while extolling the powers of the imagination. "To those devoid of imagination," Leopold writes, "a blank place on the map is a useless waste; to others, the most valuable part." For the short term, I left the ivory-billed alone and hoped that others would too.

Yet, *should* we leave the bird alone, entirely? What forms of human inter-vention are morally appropriate, required even, to ensure the survival of a species? The answer, in the case of the ivory-billed, certainly depends upon the answer to other questions raised by the sightings. Was it a single bird that had been glimpsed seven times, or multiple birds? Did a breeding pair, or several breeding pairs, exist? To open up an even bigger can of worms, how much credibility did those recent "confirmed" sightings of the ivory-billed lend, in retrospect, to the many earlier "unconfirmed" sightings over the past sixty years at various locales, including locales in Florida? The National Geographic Society's *Field Guide the Birds of North America* (1983) fairly dismisses these sightings, suggesting, "Unconfirmed sightings in recent years in Georgia, Florida, Louisiana, and Texas may actually have been the smaller Pileated Woodpecker." What are the criteria by which we gauge the credibility of knowledge claims, generally?

After several months passed, and under the supervision of a representative from the Nature Conservancy, I took advantage of a rare opportunity and traveled to Arkansas with my friend Jonathan Rosen, author of a wonderful book on birds, *The Life of the Skies* (2008), to see if we could locate the ivory-billed. We couldn't, although we hardly expected such luck after only a few days of looking. More disconcertingly, however, the sustained efforts by the Cornell Lab of Ornithology field scientists have also proven unsuccessful since the original 2004 sighting. There have been a handful of unconfirmed sightings, ranging from the highly unlikely (flitting above a parking lot near Orlando, Florida) to the more promising 2006 report published in *Avian Conservation and Ecology* documenting significant evidence (e.g., fourteen sightings, acoustical recordings, promising nesting cavity sites) that ivory-billed woodpeckers may be present in the forests in the Florida Panhandle along the Choctawhatchee River. If the ivory-billed turns up in my home state, I'll definitely seek it out, cautiously, along with Wendy and the kids.

Yet, I don't know quite how to feel anymore about the recent hoopla over the ivory-billed. I would like to believe that an especially wary few birds have managed to endure in Florida, devouring their treasured grubs from big dead trees in remote swamplands I may never visit. Yet part of me feels that this is an unreasonable (and selfish) desire, given our prominent role in their extinction. In *Hope Is the Thing with Feathers* (2000), Christopher Cokinos recounts a particularly sad and emblematic story of the last ivory-billed pair to be seen in Florida. A guide named Morgan Tindle discovered the nest in 1924 and showed it to the ornithologist Arthur Augustus Allen and his wife, Elsa. It was an incredibly exciting discovery, as many ornithologists thought the birds were already extinct. Disaster struck, however, when the Allens briefly left the nest site. "Two taxidermists," Cokinos writes, "apparently with permission from the State of Florida, shot the nesting Ivory-bills."

They've clearly had enough of us primates, the ivory-billed.

As I write these lines, however, news breaks that advances in genetic-engineering technology may make it possible sooner rather than later to resurrect various extinct species—or close versions of such species—including woolly mammoths, ground sloths, Tasmanian tigers, gastric-brooding frogs, dodo birds, passenger pigeons, Carolina parakeets, and ivory-billed woodpeckers. I wouldn't categorically oppose pursuing such efforts, yet, again, I fear that these efforts, in most cases, are at the very least premature, however well intentioned. In the case of the ivory-billed woodpecker, specifically, it seems pretty clear that we've transformed too much of their former habitat into acreage unfamiliar and hostile. It's hard to know exactly what a genetically reengineered ivory-billed woodpecker would think or do, whether they would think and do like their natural-born predecessors (which raises a whole host of additional ethical considerations). But it's probably safe to assume that their genetic memories would compel them to seek out swampland old enough to support big, long-dead trees and the juicy grubs that live in big, long-dead trees.

While we may be able to master the technology to resurrect species that have vanished, I suspect that it will prove harder for us in the United States to set aside or cultivate ecosystems to sustain these new populations. It would mean ceding to nonhuman creatures land that might otherwise be developed. It would mean giving up a larger tax base, maybe. It would mean giving up jobs, maybe. It would mean living more humbly. In short, it would take a shift in our collective values that's harder to imagine than, well, some gifted scientist figuring out in a lab how to resurrect a woolly mammoth. Perhaps we'll get there someday. But until we do, it's probably best that we let the ivory-billed woodpecker rest in peace, that we concentrate instead upon doing right by their avian cousins whom we haven't yet driven to extinction. From time to time, we might look and listen to the shockingly clear 1930s-era video footage, photographs, and audio recordings of the ivory-billed. Then, we might head outside in Florida and drink in the live sight and sound of their surviving relatives with new eyes and ears.

20

Bluefish

One fish
two fish
red fish
blue fish.
Black fish
blue fish
old fish
new fish.

FROM *ONE FISH TWO FISH RED FISH BLUE FISH*
(1960), BY DR. SEUSS

AT THE CUSP OF OUR MIDDLE AGE, and through the dazzling failure of
modern contraceptive technology, my wife and I recently found ourselves expecting our third child. After recovering from the sheer panic, I found myself
(predictably, I suppose) pondering spiritual matters for a time—the miracle
of life and all that. But mostly I thought about biology, the sheer Darwinian
doggedness of life to find its way. There were harried visits during those first
several weeks to various impeccably credentialed specialists, all of which
convinced me that we were mostly dealing with biological forces utterly
out of our control, and even our understanding. All of which scared the wits
out of me. Unlike our earlier, and deliberate, procreative efforts, the doctors
informed us that this would be a "high-risk" pregnancy, primarily on account
of my wife's relative advanced age, and secondarily on account of the more
complicated than expected surgical removal of her recalcitrant prophylactic

device. Subsequent blood tests forecasted yet a greater elevation of risk. I felt utterly without agency during the early, touch-and-go moments of my wife's pregnancy, utterly stripped of my defenses. A mere creature, suddenly.

It's probably for this reason that I found myself oddly contemplating raw creatureliness during this time. No creature, it seemed to me, better epitomized raw creatureliness than a fish I'd just started learning about, the bluefish (*Pomatomus saltatrix*). And so I found myself wanting to know even more about these mysterious animals, if only to distract myself from my tortured ruminations on the well-being of the nascent creature sharing my DNA, aswim in its own mysterious waters. When people (both Floridians and non-Floridians) think about Florida fish, they don't tend to think about bluefish. This, despite the fact that bluefish roam our offshore and nearshore waters for pretty much the entire winter, moseying down here when their northeast waters grow too cold, hewing to a yearly migration pattern similar to several of our state's retirees. While it's a prized summer game fish along the northeastern U.S. Atlantic coast, Florida saltwater anglers are distracted year-round by our piscatorial prizes deemed better looking and/or better tasting, such as mahimahi (aka dolphinfish), bonefish, blackfin tuna, snook, sea trout, redfish, and our various snappers and groupers. This is wrong.

My first experience with bluefish up close was on my friend Tim's fishing boat on a cold Florida night. We fish the reefs close to shore for yellowtail snapper, primarily, which tend to bite hard but then weaken gradually and rise to the surface upon our retrieve along a fairly straight trajectory. The mysterious creature on the other end of my line felt less aggressive at its first strike. Just heavy. I thought it was a grouper until I felt the line rise fast to the surface then veer sharply to my right. I clicked on my headlamp and fixed the beam on the line, stretched taut high above the surface for quite a ways. Several yards of line just then zipped out of my reel's drag. The creature was making the kind of run that we tend to associate with kingfish or small shark in these parts. Hammerhead, bonnethead, nurse, lemon, blacktip, spinner, and bull.

"Whoa," I cried.

"Need a gaff?" my more seasoned fishing partner asked, setting down his rod in one of the holders at the stern.

"Maybe," I uttered, as the fish tore off another stretch of line. "Maybe," in our vernacular, means "yes." Out of the corner of my eye, I saw Tim scurry to the front of the boat to retrieve our gaff from the hatch. I had deployed only a thirty-pound leader at the end of the line (we were targeting snapper), so I figured that I'd lose the kingfish or shark. But it somehow remained on the line and I was able to swing it up onto the boat without the aid of the gaff after several minutes.

"Jesus," I exclaimed. "What the heck is this?" I could tell it wasn't a kingfish right away as it was less torpedo-shaped and much thicker—over five pounds, I figured, gun-metal gray under the beam of my headlamp with a big blunt head featuring yellow eyes and an enormous jaw. It snapped its somewhat underslung jaw open and shut at a staccato pace as it hung from the line, bucking. There was something about its vigor that suggested that the landed fish wasn't yet quite convinced that between the two of us, he (or she) was the animal in trouble at the moment. I wasn't so sure, either. I stood there, frozen, contemplating my next move.

"It's a bluefish," my fishing partner told me. "Watch your fingers. It'll bite your thumb right off if you're not careful. Here, I'll get you a towel."

Voraciousness, indeed, is advertised as the bluefish's most salient feature— truly something if you think about it. Most fish, after all, eat other fish. Most of them are voracious. That bluefish have distinguished themselves in this regard suggests the downright lustful enthusiasm of their efforts. It's something that ichthyologists and common fishermen alike have noted about them from the get-go. In 1871, Professor Spencer Fullerton Baird described the bluefish as an "animated chopping machine," and the phrase stuck. The writers of the original 1902 edition of *American Food and Game Fishes* allude to Baird's description and deploy nearly poetic language to elaborate upon bluefish bloodlust:

> It has been likened to an animated chopping-machine the business of which is to cut to pieces and otherwise destroy as many fish as possible in a given space of time . . . they move along like a pack of hungry wolves, destroying everything before them. Their trail is marked by fragments of fish and by the stain of blood in the sea, as, when the fish is too large to be swallowed entire, the hinder portion will be bitten off and the anterior part allowed to float or sink. It has been even maintained that such is the gluttony of this fish, that when the stomach becomes full the contents are disgorged and then again filled!

The pack of wolves analogue (like the animated chopping-machine description) is one that recurs in separate accounts, like Rachel Carson's imaginative rendering of bluefish predation upon anchovies in her underappreciated first book, *Under the Sea-Wind* (1941). "A pack of young bluefish had picked up the scent of anchovies," Carson writes, "and swung into swift pursuit. In a twinkling they were upon their prey, fierce and ravening as a pack of wolves." Curious that writers have deployed this analogy of a land predator to describe an ocean predator. It suggests the strangeness and enduring mystery of the realm beneath the skin of the sea, below our sightline. The world we occupy, and more intimately know, is terrestrial, not aquatic. And so the terrestrial realm must serve as our frame of reference.

With regard to bluefish, specifically, there's much that we still don't know. While scientists have mostly grasped their major migration patterns, they are just beginning to determine the precise triggers, which seem to include water temperature and daylight duration. The angle of the sun apparently assists their navigation southward and northward, and some scientists have speculated that possible trace amounts of magnetite or some other mineral might aid bluefish navigation, as well. Bluefish spawning rituals remain even more mysterious—partly on account of their migration patterns, which complicate such studies—so mysterious that the authors of a 2008 article on bluefish reproduction in *Fisheries Research* could claim that "estimates of fecundity that are critical to management are almost entirely lacking for bluefish." The inscrutability of bluefish frustrates the "Stranger" character in John Hersey's *Blues* (1987), the most contemplative book on bluefish, to date. "I have been haunted, myself," the Stranger bemoans, "since I first started coming out with you, by what has seemed to me the impenetrability of the water's surface, at least by my eyes. Each time I've come out, the sea has reflected the sky as if its surface were as hard as marble, and this has made it difficult for me even to imagine what it would be like to be a bluefish, down under there."

By contrast, pondering the inscrutable sea during my wife's inscrutable pregnancy—sometimes while fishing, more often by reading—offered great comfort to me. There was something poignant about the mystery of the bluefish's very presence in Florida. While our resident snappers and groupers are fairly predictable—we pretty much know where to go on the reef to find them—we never know exactly when the first, or last, bluefish will tug on our lines come winter. Fast rovers of the open sea, they would only sporadically thump our baits throughout the season; catching one was always a jolt, nature keeping us on our toes. Thinking about these unfathomable ocean predators—the organic yet mysterious pattern to their ebb and flow in Florida—I felt, somehow, more intimately connected to the actual, unfathomable, sublime order of things, and more at peace.

There was little that I could actually do to ensure a safe pregnancy for my wife, or a healthy child at the end of the ordeal. To complicate matters further, Wendy's pregnancy coincided with the swine-flu pandemic, which had already proven lethal to a handful of pregnant women and their babies in our region. And so one concrete thing I *could* do was keep my hands, and our family's hands, clean. I stockpiled every variation of antibacterial hand sanitizer—gels, soaps, and wipes—in every corner of the house, in our cars, in our children's school-backpacks, in my school office, and on my person. I didn't realize how strange my office looked until a graduate student visited me and, crinkling her nose as she gazed about at the boxes of wipes and gel pump-bottles on my desk, declared, "You sure have lots of soap in here."

I followed the news carefully that fall as the flu outbreak radiated from public school to public school, from hospital to hospital. The swine-flu vaccine wouldn't be available until mid-October, at the earliest. While there was so much that I couldn't know or do or control about our situation, I busied myself by knowing and doing and controlling what I could.

Simultaneously, while seeking solace in bluefish mystery, I continued to learn as much as I could about them, and I continued to be impressed by accounts of their indefatigable tenacity. They came to embody for me an insatiable, creaturely enthusiasm for life, itself—life, life, and ever more life!—and offered oblique hope for our sprout, who had already overcome so much. *Be a bluefish!* I found myself praying. Fierce. Unrelenting. Indomitable.

The voracity of bluefish ought to have made the prospect of killing and eating them less disturbing to me. It's tough to feel too much pity for an animated chopping machine, a creature that cannibalizes its own slightly smaller siblings and may even kill just for the sake of killing. For years writers have referenced the fish's predilection to eat fish, and our elevated rung on the food chain, to justify our eating of fish. Ben Franklin, suffering from a pang of conscience upon the prospect of eating a cod in *The Autobiography* (1791), feels better about it after spying its entrails to notice that the fish itself had stuffed its stomach with smaller fish. Flash forward to the late twentieth century and the counsel Hersey's Fisherman in *Blues* offers to his Stranger, guilt-stricken over killing bluefish. "Try to remember that we are going after food—that we are, in a way, exploring our place in the systems of life in the universe. . . . It's what we have and must live with, at any rate."

While this all makes some sense, I couldn't help subjecting these arguments to fresh scrutiny, as raw as I felt at the time. I had already pretty much forsworn red meat, for ethical and health reasons. Now, lucky me, I was beginning to extend my scrutiny toward the killing of fish, too. Waiting for the bluefish to return that fall, I found myself wincing on my fishing outings as we went about our bloody business: cast-netting and impaling live baitfish on our hooks, allowing larger blue runners and goggle eyes to flail on deck before chopping them up for strip-bait, bringing up even larger snappers and tossing them into our coolers to suffocate. I had steeled myself against all of this. Up until then, I had (implicitly anyway) adopted the logic of Hersey's Fisherman. This was our place in the natural order of things, evidenced by our oversize crania, our very omnivore physiognomy, from our teeth to our digestive tracts. I had never extended much sympathy for the suffering of mere fish.

In my own religious tradition, the kosher laws offered me a convenient out regarding the eating of fish, particularly. While a select group of terrestrial, domesticated animals must be "slaughtered" under precise conditions (to ensure cleanliness and to minimize pain), fish, by contrast—those with scales and fins, anyway—can be "gathered" or "collected," like wheat from the fields. They don't even count as "meat," per se; they are *parve* (or neutral) and can be consumed during a "dairy" meal. Even so, fish still felt pain, I knew, as one who regularly inflicted this pain, and this suddenly bothered me. Perhaps it was only expedient, it now occurred to me, for the rabbis, and for me, to dole out our sympathies so sparingly. Fish provided protein. And fish tasted good. And fishing was fun.

But in killing and eating fish, even the most voracious among them, weren't we only animated chopping machines, ourselves? The declaration of Hersey's Fisherman about our privileged place in the systems of life suddenly seemed like an airy platitude. Shouldn't we aspire, after all, to being *better* than non-human animals? A vegan colleague of mine wears a T-shirt from time to time with lettering that reads, VEGAN, and just below, NO ONE GETS HURT. That this advertisement lately stretched across her pregnant abdomen only enforced the point for me, given my own circumstances.

Despite my crisis of conscience, I never did give up eating fish during Wendy's pregnancy. To give up fishing and eating fish would have been to give up a ritual that had grown essential to the social order of my life, the network of my human relations. It had always seemed special to prepare fish for my family—the whole process, from the catch, to the cutting board at home where I scaled, gutted, and filleted the creatures under my son's watchful eye, to the sauté pan and table, and, finally, to our backyard garden, where I buried the carcasses to fertilize our tomatoes, eggplants, and okra. Plus, I not only provided fish for my immediate family, but for two financially strapped neighbors—an elderly black woman from England, who feeds the ducks in the canals about town with great devotion, and a fifty-something Latina waitress at my favorite Cuban restaurant—both of whom greatly appreciated my surprise packages. I just couldn't give all this up.

Having decided that I would continue to catch and eat fish, the next quandary was negotiating which particular fish I should eat in Florida. Here's where bluefish came in again.

Evidence continues to mount that our insatiable western appetite for a narrowing array of fish (red snapper, grouper, and mahimahi in Florida) has provoked the overharvesting of these species and the environmentally harmful global aquaculture of species (i.e., salmon, bass) unfit for domestication. Paul Greenberg discusses this sad trend thoughtfully in *Four Fish* (2010). The Food and Agriculture Organization of the United Nations, as well, continually sounds near-apocalyptic warnings over threatened stocks of wild fish. Those of us in the United States, Japan, and the European Union are the worst culprits, according to the authors of *Fish to 2020: Supply and Demand in Changing Global Markets* (2003), as our collective consumption of high-value finfish "still dwarfs the levels in developing countries." With respect to the Florida fish triumvirate, mahimahi, given their abundance, represents the only sound environmental choice of the three, but they're bland and terrifically overrated as an eating fish if you ask me. Seafood Watch, headquartered at California's Monterey Bay Aquarium, recommends that consumers "avoid" both red snapper and grouper. Red snapper, they note, "is in decline worldwide, and fishing pressure on this species is excessive. . . . Although management measures are in place, the U.S. has not been able to prevent significant population declines of red snapper in the Gulf of Mexico." Grouper, given their brief spawning periods, are especially vulnerable to depletion. According to Seafood Watch, grouper stocks "have either been overfished or have unknown status." By contrast, bluefish, according to Seafood Watch, "are inherently resilient to fishing pressure due to their low age at maturity, moderate longevity, and high fecundity."

While the increasingly popular and inexpensive tilapia should be a good candidate for aquaculture (unlike farmed salmon, a tilapia provides more protein than it takes to cultivate), less than 10 percent of the tilapia consumed in the United States is farmed domestically. This is a problem because weak management practices in China and Taiwan, where most of our tilapia originates, release unacceptable levels of pollutants into the surrounding ecosystem. The authors of *Fish to 2020* note, staggeringly, that on account of the ongoing depletion of high-value finfish from our oceans and of our increasing reliance on aquaculture, China's share in global food-fish production, only 10 percent in 1973, "is expected to reach 41 percent by 2020."

Were our tastes more eclectic, we wouldn't be exerting such outsize fishing pressure on a dwindling number of species. But we seem more finicky than ever, especially in the United States. Most Americans favor those mildest, whitest fillets and can hardly be coaxed to eat fish whole anymore. This comes as a great surprise to most of my Trinidadian, Latino, and Afro-Caribbean friends in Florida, who wouldn't fathom forgoing the succulence of a whole fish for its measly fillet. Amid this climate, bluefish, whole or filleted, has fallen into disfavor among U.S. consumers. This is particularly frustrating for fishermen and foodies in the know, as bluefish is truly delicious, even rendering snapper and grouper bland by comparison. Sam Sifton seems befuddled in his recent food column in *The New York Times Magazine.* "It's ugly, it's oily, it happens to be delicious," he writes. "Why aren't you eating bluefish?" Here's why. To support its ravenous predation habits, bluefish (and mackerel) contain strong digestive enzymes, which leads to their quick spoilage if not gutted and iced properly. Careless fish purveyors, consequently, serve a fair share of spoiled bluefish. Wary of being on the receiving end, few Americans are willing to chance eating bluefish or mackerel.

This wasn't always so. It's interesting to explore how our eating habits have evolved over the years. "Tell me what you eat," the French gastronome Jean Anthelme Brillat-Savarin famously observed, "and I'll show you what you are." The food we put in our mouths reveals something essential not only about our chemical make-up—apparently, as Pollan argues in *The Omnivore's Dilemma* (2006), we're walking corn—but also about our shifting values and sensibilities. On this score, it seems that in the United States we've abandoned our once-intimate relationship with the food on our plate to become a nation of prima donnas. Back in 1936, Irma Rombauer's first trade edition of *The Joy of Cooking* included recipes for brains and sweetbreads, tongue and oxtails, frog legs and rabbits, goose and squab (aka pigeon), and fish of all sorts, along with detailed instructions on "cleaning" these various wild morsels. While some of our more encyclopedic cookbooks still feature instructions on how to clean fish, there's little evidence that consumers actually do so. Only commercial fishermen and fishmongers can be expected to catch and clean fish these days, while chicken and beef raised in industrial barracks and feedlots have all but supplanted our once-rich selection of domestic fowl, game, and varietal meats. In the bargain, our relationship with the food on our plate grows more distant and timid—and, I would argue, impoverished.

Perusing the literature on bluefish, specifically, one develops the distinct impression that we used to be a lot less squeamish about its sometimes strong flavor. Enthusiasm for bluefish fillets ran particularly high in my town back in the day. Milling around my university library's archives, I stumbled across a Souvenir Program for the 1967 Fiesta de Boca Raton, a multiday festival designed to promote tourism and settlement to the burgeoning community. The program's narrative advertisement for the south Florida lifestyle includes an intriguing account of the tasty bluefish along Boca Raton's shores:

> During the fall months everyone went to the beach to catch bluefish. They came south in large schools chasing the silver mullet. One school was said to have reached from Hillsboro Inlet to Jupiter. Our pioneer residents impatiently waited for the first run of bluefish, and all work was suspended on the arrival of these delicious fish. It was said one morning during religious services a man opened the church door and shouted, "The bluefish are running." The preacher pronounced a hurried benediction and rushed home for his fishing tackle, followed by the entire congregation.

These delicious fish. Few people these days use this phrase in reference to bluefish. My fellow citizens will shell out almost $20 a pound for pompano, snapper, or grouper at the store and much more than that for an entree at one of our upscale restaurants, but just try foisting bluefish (or Spanish mackerel) upon the local Florida citizenry today.

I waited anxiously, the season of my wife's pregnancy, for the bluefish to arrive in Florida, which eased my anxiety as I waited for our new child to arrive. The fish migrated southward pretty early that fall. While walking with my wife along our local pier one evening in late September, I paused to inspect the catch of a young father and his son, about thirteen or so. In addition to several gleaming lookdowns (a tasty panfish), I was surprised to notice three or four dull-gray bluefish, rubbing up against one another on the dock side-by-side like bedfellows, whereas the more plentiful lookdowns lay scattered like coins. That the bluefish were all the same smallish size is something I especially noticed, recalling reports on the parity of their individual sizes in schools given their cannibalistic tendencies.

"Get the broiler ready for those blues," I commented to the father, hoping to draw out his take on the eating quality of his bluefish catch.

"Little lemon and butter," he mused, testing the drag of his line, then smacking his lips, "Mmm-mmm." He was African American, like many of the fishermen and the fewer fisherwomen on the pier, which reaffirmed what I already knew about the less priggish tastes of American minorities and immigrants, partly on account of economic factors, when it comes to fish for food. As my wife and I moseyed farther down the pier, I noticed fresh-caught bluefish at the feet of other fishermen. We paused to observe one slender black man filleting his small bluefish with infinite care, and we chewed the fat for a while. It *was*, apparently, and as I suspected, pretty early to be catching bluefish.

The bluefish, however, weren't so quick to take *my* bait that season. Out on the water in late September and October, I thought that I was on a school of blues a few times upon suffering repeated cutoffs. Toothy creatures below. When I re-rigged with stouter tackle, however, I invariably brought up a king mackerel, if anything at all. One time I was shocked when a gleaming, silver, eel-like fish with enormous fangs rose to the surface; I released it carefully, cutting the leader with pliers as close to the mouth as I dared to reach to increase its chances of surviving. I leaned over the gunwale, watched it slither back down in the dark water toward its reef for the few seconds it remained visible beneath my headlamp. The sea continually surprises me by yielding something new and wondrous for my eyes. I had to look the creature up the next morning in Vic Dunaway's *Sport Fish of Florida* (2004). Atlantic Cutlassfish, or Ribbonfish, it was called.

As October gave way to November, as November gave way to December, I wasn't at all sure I'd catch a bluefish that season. And it seemed important that I catch at least one that winter, as much as I'd been reading and thinking about them. My wife's due date approaching, there were only so many additional nights I could risk being out on the ocean, away from home. Our summons would come soon, and heck if I'd have to explain to my child for the rest of my life why I was out fishing when he or she was born! In the meantime, I took special and unanticipated pleasure that season in attending to the most essential fishing rituals. Not the actual catching of fish, which was interesting to me, but the quieter tasks: rigging up my rods with swivels, leader, and hooks with precise knots, sharpening my filleting knives, cleaning my catch with deliberate strokes behind the pectoral, then alongside the *tat-tat-tat* of the spines, tailward, chopping onions and parsley on my cutting board as I prepared a certain fish recipe. They say that enacting simple rituals brings peace and calm during periods of stress, and I found this to be true. It's difficult to express the almost chemical comfort such exercises afforded.

If this were a story that I was writing, my hero would catch a single bluefish, and he would release it, tenderly, symbolically, just before collecting his own child from the maternity ward. But it turned out that I never did catch a bluefish that season. Some hero. I eventually gave up on the stubborn creatures, hunkered down on shore, and waited for my wife to go into labor. As she passed one pregnancy milestone after another—twenty-five weeks, thirty weeks, thirty-five weeks!—I grew increasingly amazed by the bluefish tenacity of this baby. When our child, a girl, finally sprang from her comfortable waters at thirty-nine weeks (the nurses delivered her; there was no time even to summon our doctor), I half-expected her to open her maw and bare a full set of razor-sharp bluefish teeth. But she looked every bit as frightened and frail as her siblings had looked on their birthdays, expelled from their aquatic origins: a pasting of dark hair, eyes shut tight as clamshells against the fluorescent, alien atmosphere, ears compressed, creased and folded like pie-crust rims. The only thing blue about our daughter were her feet, which took some time to gather blood. She finally wailed as the nurses tended to her, gathered in a gulp of air, wailed again, and I finally breathed too.

21

Our Suburban Screech Owls

WHEN OUR THIRD CHILD, EVA, was born, we bought a new home nearby and set about making improvements. While the larger property features eight live oaks and one laurel oak, the previous owners had crowded the understory with a dense mass of exotic flora, mostly bougainvillea (pretty specimens, but unproductive for wildlife and terribly thorny) and croton (glorified house plants). Since moving here, I've spent countless hours ripping out these exotics and planting native Florida trees and shrubs, including several specimens new to me. After several months, our gardens are finally beginning to express themselves. Fiddlewood outside my study window—yes, I've regained a dedicated study!—advertise long clusters of tiny, white flowers for the butterflies; marlberry under the oak canopy out front lick the sky with their cow-tongue leaves; delicate satinleaf flash their rusty undersides on windy days; beautyberry branches sag under the purple weight of their berry clusters, mobbed by mockingbirds and jays, and at least one summer tanager that I spotted to my slack-jawed amazement; Jamaican caper leaves beside our front patio shimmer in high-gloss when the sun catches them at dawn. And more: I've planted firebush and locustberry and wild coffee and necklace pod and bloodberry and partridge pea and sensitive plant (to replace grass) and lantana and coontie and simpson stopper and Bahama strongbark and coral honeysuckle and seven-year apple and cinnamon bark and geiger tree!

Just as I was catching my breath, Henry confronted me with his own outdoor improvement plan. "We need to build a screech owl nest box," he proposed in his characteristic terseness. The project would help him earn one of his merit badges for Boy Scouts.

"Sure," I said, because—tiredness aside—I'm all about constructive father-son activities. We scanned the Internet for building plans. This proved discouraging. Most plans included various fancy specifications: removable side panels with latches and hinges, cedar shingles for the roof replete with aluminum flashing along the sides, interior grooves outfitted with wooden slats as footholds for the fledglings, and so on. Various online video demonstrations proved equally dispiriting as they tended to feature advanced tools such as band saws, lathes, and drill-presses, none of which we owned. The whole project seemed utterly beyond the scope of our abilities.

Thankfully, we chanced upon the website of the Treasure Coast Wildlife Center, a nonprofit organization based in Palm City, Florida. Their plan for a screech owl nest box required the purchase of only a single eight-foot plank of wood, one inch thick by ten inches wide, some finishing nails, and a couple small hinges. It wasn't that I thought we'd actually be able to build it, but I figured the odds were with us that we wouldn't fail quite so spectacularly.

Megascops asio. Common name: eastern screech owl. Small owls. Seven to nine inches long. Wingspan between eighteen and twenty-four inches. Weight between five and nine ounces. Pointed ear tufts sometimes raised. Sometimes not. Dichromatic. Either gray or rufous, camouflaged with streaks, bands, or spots. Eyes yellow. Inhabits the broadest ecological niche of any North American owl. Hardwood swamps, dry prairies, mesic hammocks, mixed pine and hardwood forests, wet prairies and marshes, urban environments, pine flatwoods, sandhills, agricultural environments. Favors niches close to water. Shuns treeless expanses. Solitary, for the most part. Monogamous. Less often seen than heard. Their primary vocalization a whinny or trill or bleat or wail. Sometimes descending in pitch. But mostly monotone. Mournful, according to Roger Tory Peterson.

As Henry had decided upon a nest box for his project, it shouldn't have surprised me that he wished, specifically, to attract screech owls. As a family, we've been enamored with the creatures ever since we encountered them in our old neighborhood a few years back. My wife and I heard them before we saw them. It took us a while to figure out what it was bleating outside our bedroom window at all hours of the night, exacerbating the mild insomnia that Wendy and I have shared ever since our children were born. The sound could best be described as a high-pitched, staccato trill. It struck me as vaguely insectival.

"I think they're some kind of cicada, maybe," I uttered one still-dark morning, gazing up at the popcorn ceiling. My wife's restless shifting about beneath the covers and her exasperated exhales told me that she was awake too, listening. It wasn't such an unpleasant sound, really. Even so, it irritated me to think that it was probably just an insect. It was one thing to have our kids creep into the bedroom after a nightmare, or when they were feeling sick, or just thirsty. But a noisy bug, interrupting our precious sleep?

"Could be a frog," Wendy said. This made me feel a little better and sounded more plausible, in any case, mostly because my wife grew up in rural Pennsylvania and knows more about natural nighttime sounds.

We didn't quite know what to make of the noise outside our bedroom window, however, until we encountered owls on one of our nighttime family walks about the neighborhood. These small, strange birds. There were three or four of them darting silently back and forth from a neighbor's mailbox to what I presumed were small prey items—worms? lizards? grasshoppers?—hidden within the stiff St. Augustine grass of the front yard. We watched them for several minutes under the ochre glow of the streetlamp, long enough for me to rule them out as burrowing owls, which reside on the scruffy, undeveloped (and ever-dwindling) swatches of my university campus. Burrowing owls are slender and elongated for their small size, like gangly adolescents. These owls before us were chunkier.

"They're so adorable," our daughter Sophia whispered, clapping her hands silently beneath her chin.

"They must be screech owls," Wendy said.

The owls didn't vocalize while we observed them. They were busy performing the owl-business at hand, which required stealth rather than sound. But it didn't take us long to put two-and-two together. That mysterious nighttime bleating! When we arrived home, we scanned the Internet for screech owl sounds, which we located easily enough on the invaluable Cornell Lab of Ornithology website.

"We're such idiots," I declared, listening to the familiar staccato bleats emanating from the speakers. We hadn't even been in the ballpark with our initial guesses at the culprits keeping us up at night. Cicadas? Frogs?

Still, who would have thought screech owl? While the old neighborhood had a park full of live oaks and slash pine a block away—a parcel that the city wisely forced our subdivision developer to purchase and set aside as open space—just as close was a new and overcrowded strip-mall, its cloying restaurant smells and the glow of its artificial light a pox on us all. I-95 was nearly as close, the ceaseless hum of its traffic a sort of white noise in the background of the new, mysterious bleating. Worse, the intermittent roar of jet-planes from the nearby airport put an immediate stop to any outdoor conversation. The old neighborhood was tilting increasingly from suburban to urban. We never fathomed that something as wild as an owl could make a go of it there.

Screech owls, I had thought, belonged to the woods, agricultural fields, and lakesides of America's pastoral environs. We're a long way from this in south Florida, and in the places where most Americans now live. Around 60 percent of Americans still lived in small towns and rural villages in 1900, whereas around 85 percent of Americans now live in cities. The presence of screech owls in our suburban neighborhood seemed all the more miraculous on account of the metropolitan sprawl bearing down upon them, and upon us. For the remaining years that we lived in the old house, we continued our nighttime walks and always kept an eye and ear out for the owls. Every once in a while we spotted one perched on a mailbox, or a real-estate sign, or a storm-shutter frame jutting from a window. But mostly we didn't see or hear them.

The building plan from the Treasure Coast Wildlife Center in hand, my son and I drove to Home Depot to make our small purchases, and perhaps pick up some useful advice. We headed directly to the lumber section and walked up and down the aisle, gazing at the various planks. I finally spotted an employee wearing that telltale orange apron over his modest paunch. I asked him if he had any cedar, or cypress, or redwood, as the building plan specified, but he quickly talked me down to pine, which was all that he had. We walked over to the planks, stacked vertically, and he pulled one out for my inspection.

"You see," he said, as if I had seen something, "these planks are actually about nine inches wide and three-quarter inches thick."

When I expressed my concern that the measurements weren't precise, he explained that lumber measurements typically ran a bit short, that three-quarter inch thickness counts as one inch, for all intents and purposes.

"Oh," I said, choosing to believe him, and then, before I could check the absurdity of my next remark: "So it's sort of like a therapist's hour."

"Yeah," the man said. "Sure." The fellow looked toward Henry then, wearing an expression that can only be described as pity for the poor child, who would probably have to do without a screech owl nest box.

We picked up the rest of the materials and headed home. Per Henry's directions, I snapped a "Before" photo of him holding up the eight-foot plank in the garage.

I was feeling pretty good about things as we started in on the project. Here we were, taking up too much room as south Floridians but helping at least to enrich screech owl habitat. The shifting habitat available to screech owls in the United States is an interesting subject to contemplate. The New York City Urban Park Rangers, apparently, thought it was an uncomplicated, eco-friendly activity to reintroduce screech owls to Central Park. The screech owl plan was part of a larger project initiated in the late 1990s, dubbed Project X, to reintroduce ten plant and animal species to various New York City parks. In her fine book, *Central Park in the Dark* (2008), Marie Winn examines the story of the Central Park screech owls in some depth. The owls, she notes, had been permanent and abundant residents of the park from the time it opened until the early twentieth century. Yet, according to reliable birding surveys, they had dwindled and then disappeared by the 1950s. Why? No one in the park service seems to have studied this question before proposing to reintroduce the owls. The plan, then, while tantalizing, seemed premature to Winn and her Woodlands Advisory Board. They opposed it. They were ignored. Several individual screech owls were released in 1998 and 1999, and then again in 2001 and 2002, for a total of thirty-eight birds. The rangers even deployed the photo-op services of the lovely Isabella Rossellini for one of the releases.

Winn, who can't help but get swept up in the screech owl enthusiasm, assiduously tracks the fates of the released owls. It isn't pretty. A great horned owl preys upon at least one; squirrels and jays mob nesting cavities; one screech owl suffers a fatal skull fracture from the sharp bill of a rival screech owl; fledglings starve and decompose in a nest. The rangers emphasize that the low survival rate of their Project X owls approximates the low survival rate of screech owl fledglings in the wild. However, Winn concludes that the owls of Project X were doomed by one major variable—the automobile. She witnesses one collision between a car and an unfortunate screech owl, which swooped low after leaving its roost. While most birds leave their perch and head directly to their destination, screech owls, Winn learns, are notorious for dropping straight down and leveling off only two or three feet from the ground. She compares the historic traffic patterns in Central Park against the screech owl population trends and discovers, "The timing of screech owl extirpation in Central Park around 1950 coincides neatly with the history of car traffic there. . . . Unless cars are permanently banned from Central Park's drives, these lovely little owls will always be endangered there."

The results of Project X suggest that we can't have it all when it comes to the constructed landscape. We can't have, or expect to have, high-speed, multi-lane vehicular byways *and* screech owls.

The construction of our screech owl nest box went so smoothly that it scarcely merits discussion. Henry plotted out the proper cuts on the plank with a measuring stick and a pencil, and we set to it with our dusty electric jigsaw, which I had purchased years ago and used, I guess, for a separate project I can't recall. We placed the plank across the top of the open cupboard doors before the garage workbench. "That's not going to brace the board," Wendy warned us. But the door-tops braced the plank just fine. Henry and I took turns making the cuts. "The jigsaw isn't going to work for the diagonal cuts," Wendy predicted next. But the jigsaw sliced diagonally as smoothly as it sliced straight across. I figured, surely, that we'd split the wood at least half the time with the finishing nails, but the pine absorbed the nails without complaint. In less than an hour, we had built something that actually looked like a nest box. I drilled half-inch vent holes in the front and the bottom, but I couldn't quite bring myself to pay the twenty-odd dollars for the three-inch diameter "hole saw with arbor" to puncture the perfect-size screech owl entrance. On how many other occasions would I find myself needing to bore a three-inch hole into something? For this last part, we relied upon the well-stocked toolshed of a friend. We painted the outside of the box with a thin layer of water sealant and gave it a few hours to dry. Then I snapped an "After" photo of Henry holding the box on the driveway, a thousand-watt smile on his face. Finally, I climbed our extension ladder and used six long screws and our drill to install the box the requisite fifteen feet high against the tallest tree at our new house, a laurel oak. I was terrifically impressed that we managed to pull off what struck me as such an ambitious project until I came down off the ladder, whereupon Henry revealed that he had actually taken it easy on me, and on himself, by choosing to build something so small. His peers had mostly set their sights on much grander woodworking projects: dog houses, garden sheds, tree houses—that sort of thing.

It's curious. As soon as we put the nest box up, my investment in the creatures intensified. I wanted to know more about them, these owls who might set up housekeeping beneath our laurel-oak canopy any day now. Small wonder, I guess. It's been Wendell Berry's actual work as a farmer in Kentucky that has provoked his lifelong, thoughtful meditations upon his, and our, relationship with the land, as it was Pollan's ambitious gardening project in Connecticut that inspired his deeply philosophical early book, *Second Nature: A Gardener's Education* (1991). But this connection between active engagement and intellectual investment in the environment hit home only after I installed the nest box.

I started my research by exploring the presence of screech owls, and owls, generally, in folklore, myth, and classic literature. A symbol of Athena, Greek goddess of wisdom, the owl protected Greek armies during times of war. The owl was also guardian of the Acropolis. An owl warned the Roman army of their imminent defeat at Charrhea. Romans believed that an owl hooting presaged death. "And yesterday," one of the conspirators against Julius Caesar remarks early in Shakespeare's *Julius Caesar*, "the bird of night did sit / Even at noon-day, upon the market-place, / Howting and shrieking." Romans also feared that witches transformed themselves into owls to suck the blood of children.

Ascalphus, the son of Darkness in Ovid's Metamorphoses, is turned into a "sluggish Screech Owl, a loathsome bird." A bestiary from thirteenth-century England, translated from the Latin by Richard Barber, picks up on Ovid's loathsome theme, vis-à-vis screech owls, specifically:

> It is known as a loathsome bird because its roost is filthy from its droppings, just as the sinner brings all who dwell with him into disrepute through the example of his dishonourable behavior. It is burdened with feathers to signify an excess of flesh and levity of spirit, always bound by heavy laziness, the same laziness which binds sinners who are inert and idle when it comes to doing good.

In North America, Lenapes believed that if they dreamed of an owl it would become their guardian. The Pawnee and Sioux believed that the owl was a messenger to the first of all evil creatures. Choctaw Indians believed that the sound of a screech owl prophesied the death of a child under seven. Cherokee and Kiowa shamans saw screech owls as valued peers who could prophecy sickness. The Tlingit people of the Pacific Northwest still warn selfish girls that they might be transformed into a screech owl.

I eventually worked my way up to current field-guide entries, online reports, and Frederick R. Gehlbach's *The Eastern Screech Owl: Life History,*

Ecology, and Behavior in the Suburbs and Countryside (1994), the definitive ornithological study on the owls. Between 1967 and 1991, Gehlbach studied several nesting pairs in suburban and rural Texas: their preferred habitat, food supplies and predation, weight, coloration, molting, and breeding data. He was particularly interested in the comparative reproduction and fitness of the suburban and rural screech owl populations. What Gehlbach determined, in a nutshell, was "the suburban advantage." It turns out that eastern screech owls are especially well suited for coexistence with humans, at least in suburbia. "Modern suburbia," he writes, "is quite munificent toward this species and the few other natives that can utilize its resources." Suburbia's largesse includes relatively moderate temperatures (which enable suburban owls to begin nesting a week earlier than rural birds), a shrub density well-suited to their hunting style, ample food items—including June bugs, cicadas, earthworms, and small snakes—readily available water from sprinklers, birdbaths, and fish ponds, and, especially, few predators compared to the more hardscrabble countryside. The reduced threat of predation allows suburban owlets to remain in the nest longer, fledging at a larger, hardier size. It also keeps owlet parents alive to care for their young. Gehlbach finds that the offsetting, harmful variables of suburban living—vehicular traffic, pesticides, window-wall collisions, fewer natural tree-cavities—do not pose as great a mortality risk to the suburban owls as the extreme predation suffered by their countryside cousins.

I had assumed that screech owls thrived only in rural areas, probably because they seemed the epitome of wildness to me. The Project X results in Central Park reaffirmed this notion. But I was wrong—not only about preferred screech owl habitat but also about my simplistic notion of wilderness as mecca for all nonhuman creatures. Even my assumption that there still exists a pure wilderness, untouched by human influence, was an obsolete, romantic notion, as Bill McKibben suggests in *The End of Nature* (1989).

I learned a plethora of additional details about screech owls, most of which I'll spare you. But here's something: their unusual low flight-path to and from their nest hole—predating the invention of the automobile by eons—may have evolved at least partly to conceal their nesting site.

There's still much that we don't know about the eastern screech owl. We even had its scientific name wrong until quite recently. A note in the "Forty-Fourth Supplement to the American Ornithologists' Union *Check-List of North American Birds*," published in *The Auk* in 2003, reads, "Formerly treated as a subgenus within *Otus* . . . but mitochondrial DNA and vocal differences with Old World species indicate that generic status is warranted." And so the updated genus for the screech owl is *Megascops.* Of course, to consider this updated name the "right" name and its former scientific name "wrong" is not quite accurate. Both names, as the story of these names suggest, represent merely our best efforts to attach the most useful sign to a creature that will always evade any such attempt. One can easily imagine a time in the not-too-distant future when the entire system of taxonomy created by Carolus Linnaeus in the eighteenth century will be discredited and replaced with a new, and newly imperfect, system for identifying and organizing the earth's human and non-human creatures.

While our efforts will always come up short, there's an undeniable pleasure and privilege in the attempt, in the very act of assigning a name to a creature. In *Adam's Task: Calling Animals By Name* (1986), Vicki Hearne notes that "for us naming the animals is the original emblem of animal responsiveness to and interest in humans," as God leaves it to Adam to name the beasts of the field and the fowl of the air. Kenn Kaufman's *Advanced Birding* (1990) offers a detailed description of the screech owl trill, primarily so that we don't confuse eastern, western, and whiskered screech owls—so that we assign to each sound the proper name. Yet we probably care too much about correctly identifying and naming species and too little about everything else.

Knowing the name of the creature to associate with those mysterious trills was all I cared about for too long when we were living in the old neighborhood. It didn't occur to me to learn more about screech owls once I had identified them. I grew somewhat complacent when I still didn't really know anything. It took my nest-box project with Henry to activate my imagination, to make me wonder what those trills meant that I used to hear in the old neighborhood and that I again hear in the new neighborhood.

These trills are most common, I learn, in late winter as courtship begins, but peak again in the early fledgling period. Trilling seems to increase in advance of stormy weather. Males usually trill from specific, favored perches and upon arriving at a nest with food. They trill sporadically through the day, especially in late afternoon and early morning, while roosting near nest mates. Females may answer. Neighboring males compete with synchronous trills. Sometimes, nesting pairs engage in antiphonal trilling, or duetting. The ornithologists who wrote "The Duetting Behavior of Eastern Screech Owls" conducted mate removal and return experiments and discovered that "Paired male and female Eastern Screech owls in this study engaged in more duets during the replacement period than during the pre-removal period. . . . Such results suggest that duetting by screech owls plays a role in the establishment, or re-establishment, of pair bonds."

It's tough not to glean love in these duets. I hope to hear them soon.

Still, I should have devoted more thought to our screech owl experiment before installing the nest box in our laurel oak. Within a day of my installation of the box, my elder daughter, Sophia, alerted me to the speckled, brownish birds that she had spotted "checking out" the box. I walked outside to investigate and glimpsed a European starling enter the box with nesting material in its beak. Terrific. I waved my arms over my head and shouted like a maniac, then clapped, to scare the invader off, which worked for the moment. But I rued this unanticipated problem. As if it wasn't already bad enough that I was constantly shooing squirrels off our bird feeders, which had managed to find a workaround to our Twirl-a-Squirrel devices, now I might have to raise holy hell every day to keep the starlings out of our screech owl nest box!

Of course, as soon as I started reading about screech owls, I learned that starlings were typically among their fiercest nest-site competitors, evicting egg-laying owls in the suburbs with fair regularity. Online sources suggested that I check the nest box regularly to remove starling nesting material and eggs. One site, groping for the upside, clearly, suggested that I feed the starling eggs to my pet snake! Buying a snake to eat our starling eggs was a nonstarter. But even the prospect of climbing my extension ladder every weekend now to remove any starling nesting material unnerved me. While I'm not particularly frightened of heights, I can't say that I felt comfortable fifteen feet up.

Sophia, for her part, didn't like that I was planning on discouraging the starlings. (Henry didn't care.) "That's racist," she said. I explained that the starlings didn't belong here, that they were introduced to New York's Central Park in the late nineteenth century because some moron got it into his head that it would be a good idea to populate North America with every bird mentioned in Shakespeare's plays. Ever since, I continued, they've been bullying and out-competing our poor native bluebirds and flycatchers and woodpeckers, and screech owls too, apparently. My daughter was unimpressed with my argument.

"I value *all* living things," she answered. I couldn't think of a persuasive comeback, but I assured her that I'd check the box often to remove nesting material. That way I wouldn't have to remove any actual eggs. If I found eggs, I promised, I'd leave them alone. This seemed to satisfy her.

There was another potential problem, too, with our screech owl experiment that I hadn't anticipated. It turns out that while screech owls feed mostly on insects and other invertebrates, they also relish small birds. Gehlbach found that screech owls in the suburbs prefer resident birds to seasonal residents and migrants, and that cardinals and mockingbirds are among their most prized avian prey! Both species are abundant in my neighborhood. This is probably good for the local screech owls and goes some way toward explaining why they live here. Yet, we have taken pains to make our home a hospitable refuge for our beloved cardinals, who feast year-round at our bird feeders and plash about in the birdbath outside my study window. These lovely resident birds don't blow us off all summer, unlike some of their handsome cousins who ditch us for more temperate climes. I imagine that a few of our cardinals get taken now and again by the Cooper's hawks I see about the neighborhood. This seems fair enough. But it was another thing entirely to invite one of their chief predators to the property. I had even installed the screech owl nest box in plain sight of one of our bird feeders. While I had eagerly anticipated the prospect of our family witnessing from our dining-room window the domestic goings-on of our screech owl family, I hadn't envisioned that we might witness a father-owl, say, plucking a bright-red cardinal from the feeder with its razor-sharp talons, then returning its whole or headless body to its mate in the nest box to dismember for their owlets.

So here's what I've learned: before you do something, anything, to alter the land you live on, it's a good idea to think about the ramifications. *What animals depend upon that "nuisance" tree I'd like to cut down? What's the upside if I plant a native firebush here instead of a non-native bougainvillea? If I spray pesticide to kill the aphids on my wild coffee, what other beneficial insects might I kill? Is it worth depleting the water table to run the sprinklers today?* I try to keep the essential precept of Aldo Leopold's land ethic in mind, which he expresses pithily in *A Sand County Almanac* (1949): "A thing is right when it tends to preserve the integrity, stability, and beauty of the biotic community. It is wrong when it tends otherwise." But I didn't think about any of this before setting out to build Henry's screech owl nest. I guess it seemed to me an uncomplicated, eco-friendly activity, as Project X had probably seemed to the New York City Urban Park Rangers.

Anything we do, or don't do, on the real estate we control matters, I've come to realize—and matters in more ways than we can probably fathom. Our neighbor across the street puts out a special seed mixture to attract a noisy flock of non-native, albeit handsome, parrots. He spends much of his time screaming at the squirrels and throwing debris their way to shoo them from his parrot feeder, looking slightly more insane than I'm willing to look to discourage the rodents on my side of the street. The neighbors across the street from him, catty-corner to us, feed an outdoor tabby cat that loiters in all of our yards, devouring who knows how many parrots, cardinals, mockingbirds, and jays. My two-year-old daughter, Eva, following our mischievous example, has taken to calling the cat Evil Ginger. But she doesn't know what evil means; she likes the cat and we can't bring ourselves to discourage her affections. The neighbor beside me favors his wide-open stretch of chemically enhanced St. Augustine grass over the trees he has either chopped down or hat-racked into submission. And here we are, making our own negotiations with our modest swatch of land, which mostly entails ripping out grass, planting native trees and shrubs, and letting them grow their hair out much longer than is the current fashion. Through these various choices, we all participate in an ongoing neighborhood dialogue, mostly unspoken, on what this place ought to be, and to whom.

We've decided for now to keep the screech owl nest box. Their claim in the neighborhood likely predates ours. And they continue to live here in spite of, or on account of, its twentieth-century shift from oak and pine scrubland to suburb. Shortly after we moved to our new neighborhood, better buffered against our town's busiest byways and shopping centers, we spotted screech owls hunting in a neighbor's front yard. This is an important distinction between our small efforts to encourage screech owls here in Florida and the Project X reintroduction of the species to a locale from which they had been extirpated. As one of the designers of the first Project X release acknowledged in his 2005 study of the effort, "The most important lesson to be learned in this restoration project is that it is much easier to preserve and protect species already living in parks than it is to reestablish species once they have been eliminated." From Leopold's ethical perspective, it seems viable enough to encourage our local screech owls. It's nice to feel that the godfather of the modern environmental movement would be on our side. But mostly we just want to see them. It must be that we value the screech owls as much as, or more than, the local cardinals and mockingbirds, on whom they might dine.

We're not saddled with medieval notions of their filthiness or loathsomeness. Nor do they presage death in our eyes, as they did to certain Romans.

We think it would be nice to live in a place with owls.

The possible danger of Gehlbach's study of screech owls is that the "suburban advantage" he notes might offer us license to continue our incursions upon the countryside, in Florida and elsewhere. After all, if these "wild" and handsome screech owls like it here, we must be doing something right, yes? Yet screech owls, and parrots, and feral cats, and cardinals, and blue jays, it's worth thinking about, thrive here only at the expense of other creatures that preferred the scruffier look of the place before we imposed our neat hedgerows, well-spaced shrubs, and open expanses of grass. It's easier to see a presence than it is an absence. Even so, the screech owl's absent cousin, the great horned owl, flashes across my mental screen. This larger owl doesn't appreciate the transformed landscape on our coastal ridge, or our close company. Is it the great horned owls' fault that they can't adapt to the new environs? Their antisocial predilections, which might seem stubborn to us, served them well for millennia. Ditto for the unique behaviors of several other Florida creatures and once-creatures I've learned about and discussed in this book: snail kites, ivory-billed woodpeckers, gopher tortoises, etc. Likewise, the screech owls' low flight-path to and from their nest—ridiculously ill-suited to a nest above Central Park's West Drive—probably continues to serve them well in their rural niches.

We installed the screech owl nest box on April 21, too late in the breeding season to expect nesting this first year, I subsequently learned. April, anyway, is a sad time for us, bird-wise. Each ruby-throated hummingbird we glimpse sipping from spiked clusters of firebush blossoms might be the last we see until late September or October. Same goes for each painted bunting we spot dining at our millet feeder. In April, we welcome the sights and sounds of migrants passing through from South and Central America to points north—redstarts skittering across our live-oak branches, the occasional ovenbird skulking through our shrubs, the chimney-swift flocks giggling overhead, stubby winged cigars—but these are all fleeting, bittersweet encounters.

Meanwhile, tending our screech owl nest box has brightened my mood some. Each time I climb the ladder and check the box, I glimpse the possibility of arrival amid this season of departures. Filling the cavity with wood shavings, as one source advised, seems to have discouraged the starlings. For now. I'm only hoping that the shavings don't discourage the screech owls in the bargain. Screech owls, apparently, seek out and defend potential nesting sites throughout the year, but I haven't seen or heard evidence of them yet at our house. Instead, about half the time I've checked the box I've seen a small brown spider, nearly flat against the pine side just above the pool of wood shavings. I'm not sure if the spider's presence will discourage potential screech owl occupants or might be beneficial to the owls. Perhaps the spiders will eat mites or other bothersome owl parasites. Screech owls have been known to deposit blind snakes into their nest cavities, which serve this mutually beneficial purpose. I suspect that the small spider is a nonfactor. All I know for sure is that it's been sort of nice to open the box and see this unanticipated creature enjoying its new shelter, our project useful to some non-starling animal. It might be poisonous, I suppose. I should try to learn something about it. I should try to identify it, for starters. Soon, maybe. For now, I'm simply happy to offer the creature a wide berth.

Epilogue

An Evening Walk, December 16, 2012

AFTER SUPPER, MY FAMILY LIKES to walk around the neighborhood before settling in for the night. Short, suburban strolls. Nothing to challenge the heroic saunterings of Wordsworth, Thoreau, or Dickens, that inexhaustible urban walker. We don't manage to get out every night, and it sometimes takes a good bit of coaxing these days to motivate our two older kids, now teenagers. "Family walk!" I'll shout, or Wendy will shout, corralling Henry and Sophia. Eva, by contrast, will beat us to the door and agitate to be put in her stroller. It's a good, stress-relieving routine, escaping the indoors for the outside, and it always surprises us that we see so few of our neighbors walking, particular our neighbors with young children, particularly on our most pleasant autumn and winter nights. We'll see a few souls about (jogging, typically), but most of our suburban peers seem to avoid the outdoors as if they feared an airborne contagion.

Of course, any number of recent developments in the nation, and in my local Florida region, specifically, discourage our communion with the outdoors, from poor neighborhood planning, which demands that we hermetically seal ourselves in our automobiles to get most anywhere, to the ever-expanding arsenal of media enticements at our fingertips, to the over-air-conditioned restaurants, offices, and shopping malls, which makes the pleasant warmth of the Florida outdoors seem altogether too hot. But if there's anything that I'd like readers to come away with after reading these chapters, it's that it's worth it to expend the effort to fight these modern forces and reclaim the outside.

This isn't to say that I've managed to do so as much or as well as I'd like. Consider my evening walks with the family. We've lived here in the new neighborhood for only a few years, yet I've already noticed our tendency to let the routine become somewhat too routine. That is, left unchecked, we naturally tend to walk the exact same geometric pattern of rectangles around the various blocks, retracing our path of straight lines and right-angle turns from the night before. Our predilection to revert to autopilot, toward mindless rather than mindful walking, probably accounts, in part, for the occasional resistance of Henry and Sophia to join us. I can't blame it all on recalcitrant teenagerdom. It takes conscious and continual effort to blaze a new trail, but I've found that it's always well worth it. It amazes me how strange and wonderful a new row of trees and shrubs and gardens appears—how tantalizingly eerie the new shadows cast by moonlight through a new canopy of oaks.

So it goes for my relationship with Florida as a whole. Just when I feel like I've "done" the Everglades, or the Keys, or the Gulf or Space coast, just when a trip to a certain locale starts to feel routine, I'll visit a new area town, a new park or wildlife refuge, or simply mosey down a new path, and I'll discover that I'd only scratched the surface of a place I thought I knew so well. What's more, after my forays onto new terrain, I invariably return to those most familiar places (even our tried-and-true neighborhood walking route) with a new angle of vision. What I've learned over the years here, I suppose, is that becoming a Floridian for me has been, and will continue to be, a process of discovery, above all.

This book, then, ought not to have been read as a static catalog of the Florida phenomena that I have explored and now profess to know. Poetry, as Robert Frost claimed (and literary writing, generally), is only a "*momentary* stay against confusion" [emphasis mine]. The ephemeral nature of Frost's "stay"—a crucial element of this famous passage rarely underscored by most readers who cite it—resonates with me, particularly. These pages mostly document my first encounters with the Atlantic Ocean, the Everglades, the coontie plant, the snook, and so on. But the mind, and the writer's pen, as Frost suggests, can scarcely keep pace with the dynamic quality of life all about in the subtropics. Additional excursions continue to reveal new dimensions to these Florida phenomena. Each birding trek to the Everglades yields new discoveries; each season with my vegetable garden is a new adventure; I'm drawn back time and time again to fish just outside my local inlet at night because I never fish the same ocean. Provided we take better care of the state over the next hundred years than we have for the past hundred years, we will be rewarded with its limitless and ever-surprising beauty. I suspect that the same might be said for the other forty-nine states. But I live in Florida.

We enjoyed a particularly nice walk around the neighborhood last night. We almost didn't go, as I was busy setting up a portable sprinkler to irrigate a dry patch of our garden out front. Everyone else was busy enough inside, I suppose. But then I heard what I thought were the distant bleats of a screech owl. The monotonic trill seemed to be coming from the Northeast, several blocks away. It's always a special treat to hear or see screech owls in the neighborhood, so I rushed into the garage and swung open the door to the family room. "Come on, everybody!" I shouted inside. "Time for a walk. I hear an owl!" Thankfully, owl-news qualifies as exciting to my wife and kids, particularly since Henry and I built and installed our screech owl nest box. We were on our way within minutes.

We walked for several blocks in the direction in which I thought I heard the call, but the darn owl hushed up, as if it knew we were out to find it and wished to conceal itself. It might have been that we simply couldn't hear the bleats anymore below the din of the holiday music, which some of my neighbors play in syncopation with their blinking holiday lights. The unusual number of cars roaring up and down the street on this particular evening wasn't helping any, either. We enjoyed the walk, in any case, which took us to northern blocks that we only rarely venture to. Before turning back, I wanted to head up one more block all the way to the last, narrow street in our neighborhood, a one-way street bordered by a drainage canal and untrimmed foliage. On breezy nights, these untrimmed branches will grind and squeak against one other, spookily. I have a theory (unproven) that any number of our neighborhood raptors roost in the sea grape, oak, palm, and pine in this dark, quiet borderland between neighborhoods, but my wife has a theory (proven, more or less) that a larger number of mosquitoes also congregates along this strip. We headed back, conceding defeat.

No sooner did we walk up our drive, however, than I heard the lovely screech owl trill once again, tantalizingly close. "*Shhh*, you hear that?" I whispered. The owl trilled again. We all heard it. It seemed to be perched somewhere just overhead! Additional bleats revealed that it was in our largest live oak, beside the driveway. We couldn't see it in the dark, but we stood there, frozen, for several minutes, relishing the serenade. Even our youngest, Eva, sat

Screech-owl nesting in Henry Furman's nest box, March 3, 2013.

quietly in her stroller. The owl, likely a male, had, I hoped, found our nest box
in the adjacent laurel oak, whose fingers interlock with the live oak's fingers
high above in our front-yard canopy. The creature was calling, perhaps, to advertise its new homestead for its mate, or for potential mates. I imagined that
it was the same bird that I had heard off in the distance, earlier—that while
we zigzagged through the neighborhood in pursuit, the owl had followed its
own circuitous path through the patchwork of neighborhood trees, beating its
silent wings just over our heads, maybe. Here it was now, to welcome us back
to the home we all shared.

Acknowledgments

FOR THEIR HARD WORK on behalf of this book, I would like to thank Amy Gorelick and Meredith Morris-Babb at the University Press of Florida. I would also like to express my appreciation to the following people, who have supported this book in various ways: the anonymous readers of the press, who offered helpful comments and suggestions; my colleague, Papatya Bucak, who offered invaluable feedback on a late draft of this book, and all of my talented colleagues in the Department of English at Florida Atlantic University; Tim Lenz, Robert Stone, and the late Jack Freeman, for their piscatorial, avian, and arboreal expertise, respectively; and, of course, my wife, Wendy, and our children, Henry, Sophia, and Eva.

Several of these chapters, or significant material from them, were originally published elsewhere: in *ISLE: Interdisciplinary Studies in Literature and Environment*, "The Tale of a Cuban Immigrant," 10.2 (Summer 2003): 147–54; "A Trip to Venus," 14.1 (Winter 2007): 191–202; and "The Field of the Microscope," 20.3 (Summer 2013): 657–69; in the *Oxford American*, "Live Oak," published as "Big Wood," 70 (2010); in *The Chronicle of Higher Education*, "Ivory-Billed Woodpecker," published as "The Miraculous Sighting of a Vanished Bird" (June 3, 2005), and "Thoreau in Florida," published as "Thoreau in the Everglades" (August 16, 2002); and in *Agni Online*, "Snooking" (December 11, 2009). I am grateful to the editors of these journals and magazines for their support of my work and for their reprint permission.

Appendix

Florida Flora and Fauna: A Selected Checklist

BIRDS

snail kite
northern harrier
short-tailed hawk
sharp-shinned hawk
peregrine falcon
Cooper's hawk
osprey
merlin
swallow-tailed kite
white-tailed kite
burrowing owl
eastern screech owl
great-horned owl
northern parula
black-throated blue warbler
prairie warbler
yellow-throated warbler
common yellowthroat
American redstart
bay-breasted warbler
ovenbird
Cape May warbler

pine warbler
palm warbler
black-and-white warbler
white-eyed vireo
blue-headed vireo
black-whiskered vireo
red-eyed vireo
black-capped chickadee
eastern pewee
smooth-billed ani
boat-tailed grackle
Cuban pewee
great crested flycatcher
La Sagra's flycatcher
white-crowned pigeon
Key West quail dove
mourning dove
common ground dove
white-winged dove
Eurasian collared dove
chimney swift
blue-gray gnatcatcher

spot-breasted oriole

northern cardinal

blue jay

northern mockingbird

brown thrasher

Florida scrub-jay

summer tanager

eastern towhee

eastern bluebird

eastern meadowlark

Bachman's sparrow

painted bunting

snowy egret

wood stork

green heron

great blue heron

roseate spoonbill

limpkin

white ibis

Florida sandhill crane

tri-colored heron

little blue heron

common moorhen

American coot

pied-billed grebe

great egret

greater shearwater

northern gannet

magnificent frigatebird

royal tern

brown pelican

crested caracara

red-cockaded woodpecker

red-headed woodpecker

red-bellied woodpecker

pileated woodpecker

yellow-bellied sapsucker

yellow-billed cuckoo

Carolina wren

MAMMALS

wild boar

red Fox

opossum

raccoon

eastern gray squirrel

fox squirrel

Key Largo woodrat

Key Largo cotton mouse

Florida mouse

bobcat

river otter

armadillo

striped skunk

REPTILES

gopher tortoise

loggerhead turtle

leatherback turtle

green turtle

eastern indigo snake

FISH

common snook	mahimahi (aka dolphinfish)
cobia	lemon shark
wahoo	bull shark
yellowtail snapper	black-tipped shark
mangrove snapper	hammerhead shark
mutton snapper	bonnethead shark
king mackerel	nurse shark
bluefish	

BUTTERFLIES

monarch	Gulf fritillary
queen	julia
soldier	ruddy daggerwing
gold-rimmed swallowtail	common buckeye
giant swallowtail	white peacock
Schaus' swallowtail	Florida white
orange sulphur	great southern white
cloudless sulphur	mangrove skipper
zebra longwing	silver-spotted skipper
atala	

LARGE TREES

live oak	royal palm
laurel oak	slash pine
water oak	sand pine
gumbo limbo	longleaf pine
citrus	strangler fig
geiger	magnolia
coconut palm	cypress
Sabal palm	mahogany

SMALL TREES AND SHRUBS

Bahama strongbark
beautyberry
cinnamon bark
cassia
coral honeysuckle
locustberry
sensitive plant
partridge pea
seven-year apple
Jamaican caper
firebush
fiddlewood
marlberry
bloodberry
sawgrass
satinleaf
wax myrtle

wild coffee
saw palmetto
cabbage palmetto
Simpson's stopper
bromeliads
plumbago
Spanish moss
ball moss
coontie
lantana
golden dewdrop
necklace pod
Florida privet
long strap fern
Curtis' milkweed
banded air plant
large-flowered rosemary

Selected Further Reading

Alden, Peter, and Rick Cech. *National Audubon Society Field Guide to Florida*. New York: Knopf, 1998.

Ambrose, Holly. *30 Eco-Trips in Florida: The Best Nature Excursions (And How to Leave Only Your Footprints)*. Gainesville: University Press of Florida, 2005.

Audubon of Florida: http://fl.audubon.org/

Belleville, Bill. *Salvaging the Real Florida: Lost and Found in the State of Dreams*. Gainesville: University Press of Florida, 2011.

Douglas, Marjory Stoneman. *The Everglades: River of Grass*. 1947. Sarasota, Fla.: Pineapple Press, 1997.

Dunaway, Vic. *Sport Fish of Florida*. Palm Coast, Fla.: Wickstrom Publishing, 2004.

Friend, Sandra. *Hiker's Guide to the Sunshine State*. Gainesville: University Press of Florida, 2005.

Gilman, Edward F., Robert J. Black, and Sydney Park Brown. *Your Florida Guide to Shrubs: Selection, Establishment, and Maintenance*. 2nd ed. Gainesville: University Press of Florida, 2013.

Glassberg, Jeffrey, Marc C. Minno, and John V. Calhoun. *Butterflies through Binoculars: A Field, Finding, and Gardening Guide to Butterflies in Florida*. New York: Oxford University Press, 2000.

Grunwald, Michael. *The Swamp: The Everglades, Florida, and the Politics of Paradise*. New York: Simon & Schuster, 2006.

Haehle, Robert G., and Joan Brookwell. *Native Florida Plants: Low-Maintenance Landscaping and Gardening*. Lanham, Md.: Taylor, 2004.

Huegel, Craig N. *Native Plant Landscaping for Florida Wildlife*. Gainesville: University Press of Florida, 2010.

Klinkenberg, Jeff. *Seasons of Real Florida*. Gainesville: University Press of Florida, 2009.

Larson, Ronald J. *Swamp Song: A Natural History of Florida's Swamps*. Gainesville: University Press of Florida, 1995.

Maehr, David S., and Herbert W. Kale II. *Florida's Birds: A Field Guide and Reference*. Sarasota, Fla.: Pineapple Press, 2005.

Myers, Ronald L., and John J. Ewal. *Ecosystems of Florida*. Gainesville: University Presses of Florida, 1990.

Opler, Paul A. *Eastern Butterflies*. New York: Houghton Mifflin, 1998.

Peterson, Roger Tory. *A Field Guide to the Birds*. 1934. New York: Houghton Mifflin, 1980.

Pranty, Bill. *A Birder's Guide to Florida*. Asheville, N.C.: American Birding Association, Inc., 2005.

Rawlings, Marjorie Kinnan. *Cross Creek*. 1942. New York: Scribner, 1996.

Ray, Janisse. *Pinhook: Finding Wholeness in a Fragmented Land*. White River Junction, Vt.: Chelsea Green, 2005.

Sibley, David Allen. *The Sibley Field Guide to Birds of Eastern North America*. New York: Knopf, 2003.

Sierra Club Florida: http://florida.sierraclub.org/

Stowe, Harriet Beecher. *Palmetto Leaves*. 1873. Gainesville: University Press of Florida, 1999.

Sunquist, Fiona, Mel Sunquist, and Les Beletsky. *Florida (Travellers' Wildlife Guides)*. Northampton, Mass.: Interlink Books, 2007.

Taylor, Walter Kingsley. *Florida Wildflowers in Their Natural Communities*. Gainesville: University Press of Florida, 1999.

The Nature Conservancy: http://www.nature.org/

Walton, Dan, and Laurel Schiller. *Natural Florida Landscaping*. Sarasota, Fla.: Pineapple Press, 2007.

Whitney, Ellie, D. Bruce Means, Ann Rudloe, and Eric Jadaszewski. *Priceless Florida: Natural Ecosystems and Native Species*. Sarasota, Fla.: Pineapple Press, 2004.

ANDREW FURMAN is professor in the Department of English at Florida Atlantic University and teaches in its MFA in creative writing program. He is the author, most recently, of the memoir, *My Los Angeles in Black and (Almost) White*. His work has appeared in such publications as *Oxford American*, *Ecotone*, *Poets & Writers*, *Agni Online*, *The Chronicle of Higher Education*, *ISLE*, and the *Miami Herald*.

THE UNIVERSITY PRESS OF FLORIDA is the scholarly publishing agency for the State University System of Florida, comprising Florida A&M University, Florida Atlantic University, Florida Gulf Coast University, Florida International University, Florida State University, New College of Florida, University of Central Florida, University of Florida, University of North Florida, University of South Florida, and University of West Florida.